TIGER BOOKS INTERNATIONAL

past and present

PARIS

Text
Milena Ercole Pozzoli

Editing Supervision
Valeria Manferto De Fabianis

Art Director
Patrizia Balocco

Graphic design
Anna Galliani
Alberto Bertolazzi
Clara Zanotti

Translation by
Neil Frazer Davenport

1 In this unusual shot, the Eiffel Tower is framed between the obelisk from Luxor and one of the many statues that grace the famous Place de la Concorde.

2-7 The Palace of Versailles is enhanced with magnificent fountains and sculptures.

3-6 An aerial view of the Seine, the celebrated river flowing through Paris

along the banks of which the city's intense trading activities were concentrated up until the end of the 17th century.

7 The severe facade of Notre-Dame rising into the Parisian sky.

This edition published in 1997 by TIGER BOOKS INTERNATIONAL PLC , 26a York Street Twickenham TW1 3LJ, England.

First published by Edizioni White Star.
Title of the original edition:
Parigi.
© World copyright 1997 by Edizioni White Star,
Via Candido Sassone 22/24, 13100
Vercelli, Italy.

ISBN 1-85501-904-3

Printed in Italy by Grafedit, Bergamo (Italy).
Colour separations by Fotomec, Turin (Italy).

CONTENTS

jects, whilst at the same time a *grande dame* ever capable of provocation and seduction. However, Paris is above all a state of mind, an imaginary world, a great unspoilt dream, a living legend that conquers with its sudden, tentacular hold over the senses. It is a capital of the world and of the spirit. Fundamentally we visit Paris on the pretext of the new in order to be reassured as to the fact that the old is unchanged, and it is on the subtle boundary between past and present that we find the eternity and uniqueness of this metropolis. In contrast with other capitals that resemble geological strata, Paris blends its past and future: the seventeenth-century quarters and the Défense, the Louvre treasure-chest and the challenge of the glass pyramid, the great boulevards and the heavily criticised Opéra-Bastille. If there is a city in the world that can boast of always having been a cradle of the avant-garde, that city is Paris. Here were born the most violent of political, cultural, artistic and social revolutions, from the Reformation to the Can-Can, from Cubism to the civil unrest of 1968, from fashion to architecture to the cinema. Almost all the writers and painters who count from the mid-nineteenth century onwards have lived and dreamed in Paris; no other city in the world can claim as much.

Brilliant and adventurous lives have been consumed on every street corner, have inhabited Bohemian attics and sumptuous palaces, have wept, laughed, loved, suffered and above all written chapters, exposed kilometres of celluloid, sculpted faces and painted canvases that have become pages in the very history of the city itself. It was here that in just fifty-two days Stendhal wrote *La Chartreuse de Parme*; it was here that Picasso lived and worked; Modigliani found a house in Rue Delta in

10 The bull's head and the dog of Paul Jouve, the gilding glittering in the sun, adorn the Trocadero fountain.

10-11 This stunning photograph, taken from the Arc de Triomphe shows Paris as the sun sets.

12-13 The Pont Alexandre III is a Parisian jewel, gilded and grandiose in accordance with the seductive stylistic canons of the Belle Époque. No less than 17 artists worked on its decoration and the foundation stone was laid by Tzar Alexander II, although it was his successor who saw the completion of the great work and to whom it was dedicated in a solemn inauguration ceremony in 1900.

14-15 *When it was erected it was a source of scandal, but a hundred years on, the Eiffel Tower, an attraction built for the 1889 World's Fair, is so much a part of the Parisian landscape as to be the symbolic hub around which the whole city revolves. In this image the Iron Lady appears by a trick of perspective to be rising from the roofs of the city.*

Montmartre and later in Montparnasse. In the church of Saint-Roch, Alessandro Manzoni saw the light and decided on his conversion; Casanova lodged in Rue de Tournon, Goldoni died in Rue Dussoubs and Chopin breathed his last in a white palace close to Place Vendôme.

Paris is the city where reality and literature have always met as if in the suspended universe of a dream. Together with the ghosts of authors, the streets are roamed by the spirits of characters that came into the world thanks to their pens, spirits that carry with them a world of pure imagination. They go in and out of houses, they wander the banks of the Seine, linger in the yellow lamplight of Parisian nights and whisper among the lime trees of Saint-Germain-des-Près. They too are an integral part of the atmosphere of Paris, along with a sensation that the city is holding something special in store for you, an adventure, a surprise, a favour, an emotion. From her faded rooftops, dotted with chimneys, from her romantic parks, from the top of the Eiffel Tower or from a stroll along the bridges of the Seine, Paris reveals the myriad facets of her popularity and offers the fullness of her appeal to tourists and residents alike. Whilst Paris retains its mysteries and is the ideal city of folly, she is also a futuristic capital of telecommunications, a city that lives according to frenetic rhythms and exploits every last square centimetre of space, a city of the ephemeral and exorbitant prices. After all, what modern metropolis does not exist through perennial contradictions?

The difference is that Paris possesses the exclusive weapon of total seduction and unconsciously infects us all with its eternal and irrepressible *joie de vivre*.

16-17 *This evocative aerial photo allows us to admire the old street plan and the principal monuments of Paris. In particular the Ile de la Cité and the Ile Saint-Louis, the historic heart of the city, can clearly be seen.*

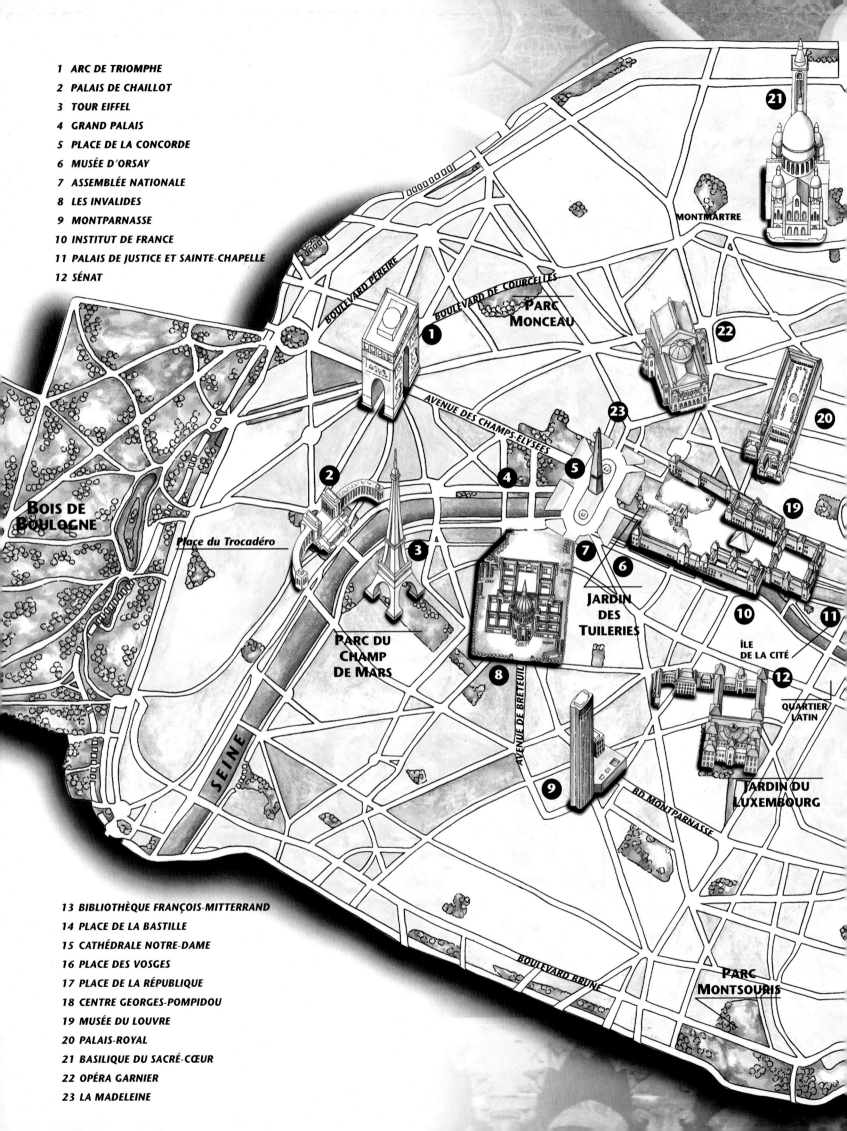

BOULEVARD PÉREIRE

BOULEVARD DE COURCELLES

PARC MONCEAU

MONTMARTRE

AVENUE DES CHAMPS-ELYSÉES

BOIS DE BOULOGNE

Place du Trocadéro

PARC DU CHAMP DE MARS

SEINE

JARDIN DES TUILERIES

AVENUE DE BRETEUIL

ÎLE DE LA CITÉ

QUARTIER LATIN

JARDIN DU LUXEMBOURG

BD MONTPARNASSE

BOULEVARD BRUNE

PARC MONTSOURIS

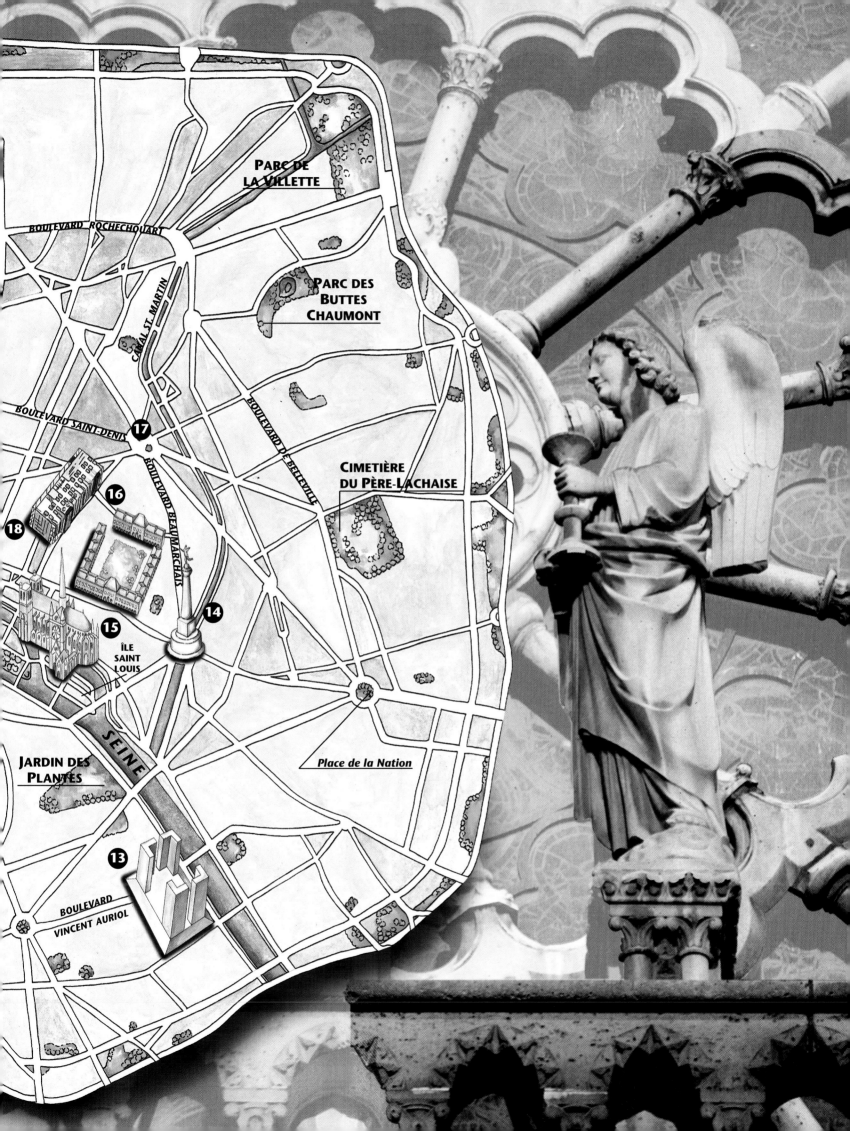

PARC DE
LA VILLETTE

BOULEVARD ROCHECHOUART

PARC DES
BUTTES
CHAUMONT

CANAL ST. MARTIN

BOULEVARD SAINT-DENIS

BOULEVARD DE BELLEVILLE

17

16

18

BOULEVARD BEAUMARCHAIS

CIMETIÈRE
DU PÈRE-LACHAISE

14

15

ÎLE
SAINT
LOUIS

SEINE

JARDIN DES
PLANTES

Place de la Nation

13

BOULEVARD
VINCENT AURIOL

ETERNAL GRANDEUR

Jewels, vases, furnishings, necklaces, axes, daggers, statuettes and many other artefacts have been recovered thanks to archaeological excavations over the last two hundred years that have allowed us to reconstruct the decisive phases in the development of Paris. The legendary Roman *oppidum* has revealed many of its secrets: the

20 top left Over the centuries the birth of Paris has inspired engravings, prints, paintings and bas-reliefs.
This illustration shows part of ancient Lutetia, *taken from an engraving published in* Paris à travers les siècles, *by the historian G. de Genouillac.*

20 bottom left and top right The first inhabitants of what in time was to become the legendary Ville Lumière *were the Parisii, a rough, primitive people as seen in these engravings showing men and women engaged in daily chores.*

location of the principal streets, the foundations of the *forum*, the remains of the *capitolium*, the theatre and the arena. In the quarter of Bercy in the 13th arrondissement, the building of an underground car-park brought to light a Neolithic village following the discovery of a number of wooden canoes and 250 bronze age vases; it was excavations along the Rue Pierre-et-Marie-Curie that revealed the secrets of a Gallic-Roman kiln found almost intact, whilst the subsoil of Notre-Dame has given up, at least in part, the pillars of the temple of Tiberius, erected on behalf of the boatsmen's guild in the middle of the first century B.C.

Digs around the Latin quarter have also helped to complete our picture of ancient *Lutetia*, the Gallic-Roman village built on the foundations of the primitive village inhabited by the Parisii tribe. In the year 52 B.C. one of Julius Caesar's centurions arrived to challenge the Gaul Camulogenus close to this settlement, composed of simple huts on an island in the middle of the Seine. A full-scale war was fought that led to the destruction of the Gauls. The Roman settlement of *Lutetia* was then raised on the remains of the ancient village on the cradle-shaped island now known as the Ile de la Cité. The principal axis was oriented along the approximate route of what is today Rue Saint-Jacques and the decuman probably led straight to the boats moored along the banks of the Seine.

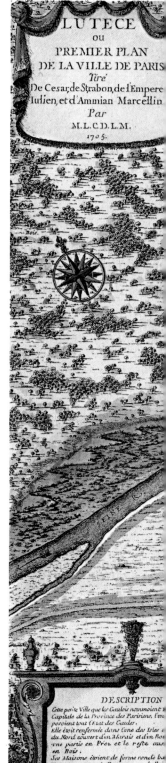

21 top In Paris à travers les siècles *by G. de Genouillac, published in 1878, there are depictions of the early Gauls and the horsemen of the first century AD who inhabited what was to become Paris.*

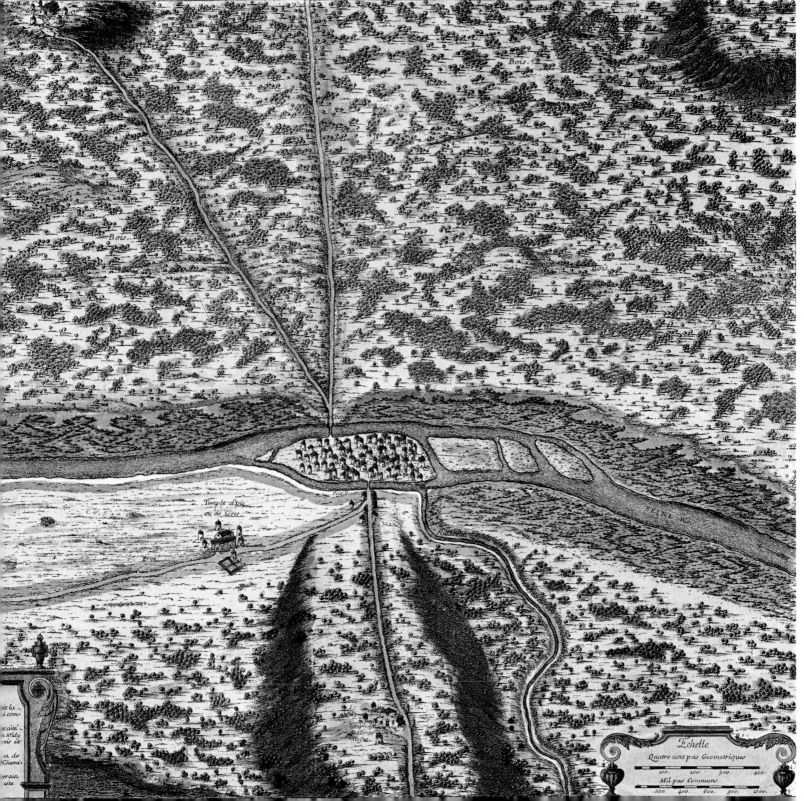

This was to all intents and purposes the birth of Paris. "The gravel beach of that island was its first city wall, the Seine its first moat" wrote Victor Hugo in *Notre-Dame de Paris*. He went on to add, "For a number of centuries Paris remained an island, with two bridges, one to the North, the other to the South and two bridgeheads that served her as both ports and fortresses, the Grand-Châtelet on the right bank and the Petit-Châtelet on the left. Then, from the epoch of the kings of the first dynasty, Paris, feeling constrained on her island on which there was no longer space in which to move, decided to cross the river. Beyond the larger and smaller Châtelets a first turreted wall of stone began to enclose the countryside on either side of the Seine... little by little the tide of houses, thrust out from the heart of the city towards the periphery, broached, eroded and erased that first wall." The sequence of civil wars and the barbarian invasions did little to prevent Rome from extending its control for many centuries over these lands and much of France. In 250 the first bishop Saint-Denis died as a martyr on, as legend would have it, the hill that would later become known as Montmartre, but Christianity nevertheless spread through the small community.

23 left The first of a series of barbarian raids by the tribes from beyond the Rhine began in 275. Faced with this threat Paris retreated within the well fortified Cité. Nevertheless, Attila, the Scourge of God, as noted in this illustration taken from a 12th-century painting, besieged the city in 451.

23 right At this point legend takes over from history: it is said that thanks to the divine intervention implored by the young Geneviève, seen here in an illustration by Lion Royer from Le Petit Journal, the fearsome Attila turned his back on the city and departed for the South without sacking it.

ATTILA FLAGEL:DEI

From 275 onwards the threat of barbarian invasions represented a severe test of the defences of the *oppidum*. In the fourth century the already densely populated fortified city was protected by the fleet of Roman ships moored on the Seine, a small but well-armed garrison and massive city walls. For over a century the houses clambered one on top of the other and the streets became increasingly narrow, imprisoned within the ring of tall, solid towers. In the fifth century, Paris was thus able to put up stubborn resistance to the siege of Attila the Hun, backed by the divine intervention of young Geneviève who convinced the besieged population to pray. As if by a miracle, Attila completed an about turn and left with his army heading south. *Lutetia*, by now known as Paris, was safe and Geneviève was later canonised and proclaimed as the patron saint of the city. A slim statue in pale marble depicting her still dominates the Pont de la Tournelle.

23

24 top These helmeted and armoured warriors from the era of the alliance between the Franks and the Gauls give an idea of the customs and costumes of Merovingian Paris. Soon after he was declared King, Clovis transferred the capital of his kingdom to the banks of the Seine.

24 centre left Victorious at Soissons over the troops of the Roman Empire, Clovis (481-511) became master of Gaul, converted to Roman Catholicism and was proclaimed King of the Franks and crowned as such in Reims cathedral, as can be seen here in an illustration taken from Les Grandes Chroniques de France.

24 centre right Taken from Paris à travers les siècles, *this engraving shows Clovis being carried in triumph by his men.*

24 bottom This illustration from 1541 depicts the coronation of King Pepin by St. Boniface in 751.

25 top Charlemagne only briefly resided at Paris, preferring Rome or Aix-la-Chapelle to the city on the Seine. In this painting by Julius Schorr von Carlosfeld he is seen entering Paris in triumph.

Late in the fifth century the history of the Salian Franks was unified with that of Roman Gaul. Clovis, victorious at Soissons against the troops of the Roman Empire, became King of Gaul. He married the Christian Clotilda who persuaded him and his army to convert to her religion. He was crowned King of the Franks (from whom the name of the country derives) at Reims in 508 and transferred the capital of his kingdom to the banks of the Seine. In this period Paris was dotted with half-built churches, nine in construction on the left bank and three on the right. Clovis ordered the construction of the church dedicated to the Apostles where he wished to be buried and where some time later the remains of Saint Geneviève were also interred. A son, Childebert, who was to reign for 47 years, commissioned the building on the same bank of the Seine of an immense basilica, the largest in Merovingian Gaul and another that housed the remains of St. Germain, the bishop of Paris late in the sixth century, on the foundations of which the St. Germain-des-Prés abbey was built.

25 bottom left
In 751, following
the deposition
of Childeric III,
the last Merovingian
king, Pepin the Short
and then Charlemagne
were crowned as King.
Charlemagne is seen
here in regal dress
and with the symbols
of power in his hands
in a celebrated portrait
by Albrecht Durer.
The King subsequently
left Paris defenceless
and late in the 9th
century it was sacked
on a number of
occasions by the
Normans. The Cité
resisted a long siege,
but nothing remained
of the Roman Paris
of the Rive Gauche.

25 bottom right
This 15th-century
engraving shows
the Ile de la Cité in
the era of
Charlemagne. As you
can see the city was
already notably well
developed.

The Merovingians conquered almost all of Roman Gaul, but with the advent of the seventh century, civil disorder, the undisciplined court life, the lack of a political policy, the division of the kingdom and internal strife among the rulers, led to the decay of the dynasty and the rise of Pepin the Short and the Carolingians. In 751 the last Merovingian King Childeric III was deposed by Pepin who himself took the title of King. When his son Charlemagne came to the throne, he established the capitals of his kingdom at Rome and Aix-la-Chapelle and was rarely resident in Paris. Hard times beckoned as the city was abandoned by the last of the Carolingians; during the ninth century it was sacked by Norman adventurers. The outskirts were destroyed and as Paris retreated within the confines of the Cité the last traces of the Roman *oppidum* disappeared.

In 987 Hugh Capet of the Capetian dynasty entered the scene and, as it approached its first millennium, Paris, with its wealthy abbeys, its annual fair and its markets, reassumed its role as capital of the kingdom. Louis VI "the Large" (1108-1137) established his residence in a palace on the Cité, the original island that was increasingly crowded with houses. In 1163 Bishop Maurice de Sully began the construction of Notre-Dame on the site of the old Merovingian church and in 1180 Philip Augustus once again imprisoned the city within a new ring of fortified walls with tall, powerful towers; in order to cope with the assaults of the King of England he built the Louvre fortress that was soon to serve as a royal residence and gave new impulse to the Les Halles de Champeaux, the celebrated Paris market established by Louis the Large and that was to remain in situ for eight centuries. Bianca of Castile, the wife of Philip Augustus, commissioned the building of Sainte-Chapelle. Within a few decades even the new city walls proved unable to allow for the expansion of the city that was by now composed of fourteen parishes. Medieval Paris developed on the right bank of the Seine and was a major centre on the great trading and communications routes. Textiles from Flanders arrived along Rue St.-Denis, grain along Rue Saint-Honoré and the fish from Normandy and Brittany arrived in the city along Rue des Poissoniers. The Seine, the most natural and immediate means of communication for all trade, was by now the scene of a constant bustle of barges and boats. "The houses breached the walls of Philip Augustus", wrote Victor Hugo, "and happily scattered across the plain with neither order nor symmetry as if they had escaped from a prison. Once there they dug a garden in the fields and sat at their ease". The origins of the Parisian suburbs lie in this period and are linked to the expansion of the inhabited areas around the first urban parishes such as Saint-Germain l'Auxerrois, Saint-Merry, Saint-Jacques-la-Boucherie and Saint-Nicolas-des-Champs. In contrast, the left bank was almost completely abandoned. The slopes of the Sainte-Geneviève hill became agricultural land owned by the monks of the great abbeys such as the nearby and already flourishing Saint-Germain-des-Prés.

Under St. Louis IX, the aristocracy was weakened by the crusades in the Holy Land and against the Cathars. The university, instituted and recognised by a Papal Bull issued in 1209 by Pope Innocent III, ensured that the city enjoyed international prestige as a centre of learning. In 1257 Robert de Sorbon founded the university for the teaching of theology, law, art and medicine that was to take his name. When he came to the throne Charles V ordered the construction of the Bastille and city walls on the right bank to enclose the new quarters. Once again, however, these soon proved inadequate in the face of the continued rapid expansion of the city. Thus it was that by the fifteenth century Paris extended far beyond the concentric rings of fortifications that since the era of Julian the Apostate had attempted to restrain her within their defensive patterns.

28 left St. Louis IX, depicted while visiting Notre-Dame accompanied by his mother Bianca of Castille; according to Jacques Le Goff "he was a sainted knight, a sainted warrior. The King applied the two great rules of Christian war, of right and just war, whilst continuing to serve the interests of the French monarchy." The category to which St. Louis belonged was that of the lay saints. In terms of politics he attempted to be an ideal Christian king whose virtues were manifested through power, wisdom and goodness.

28 right This painting shows St. Louis in front of the church of John the Baptist; in the background can be seen the towers of Paris.

29 Charles V, "The Wise", seen here in a portrait by Orley Bernard was an able financial strategist and skilfully reorganised the army. Having reopened the war with the English he managed to reduce their possessions to a few coastal fortresses. When he was still the Dauphin, however, he had had to tackle the first Parisian revolt led by Etienne Marcel, the spokesman for a discontented populace. Having come to the throne following the execution of Marcel, Charles carried with him the memory of those signals of fracture between sovereign power and the capital and the first thing he did was to leave the Ile de la Cité (top left), order the building of the Bastille and complete the construction of a new city wall on the Right Bank that, following the course of the Seine, was set at a right-angle to the present-day Carrousel. The Louvre (bottom) ceased to be a fortress and began to be meticulously transformed by Charles V into a royal palace. He had the building heightened, enriched with windows, decorated with statues and embellished internally. He placed his rich library in the northwest court and his collection of works of art in the large halls. He also ordered the planting of lush gardens with porticoes and pavilions.

The fourteenth century was a difficult period for Paris. In 1348 it was struck by the Black Death, a plague that decimated the population of 200,000 souls. What was worse was that the struggle for the French throne between the Capetians and the English king Edward III of the Plantagenet dynasty sparked off the Hundred Years War (1337-1453). The war did, however, bring to an end a series of civil disorders provoked by legendary demagogues such as Simon Caboche and Capeluche who threw Paris into a climate of terror between 1413 and 1418. On the death of Charles VI, the Dauphin and future King Charles VII fled the peril of rebellion by seeking refuge at Bourges, giving rise to that period of gilded exile that saw the banks of the Loire with their enchanted castles adopted as the "capital" of the kingdom. The English entered Paris in 1420, on the death of Charles VI, and proclaimed Henri VI of England as the King of France despite his tender age. Just as victory appeared to be within the

30 bottom *This 15th-century miniature depicts a battle between knights on horseback during the Hundred Years War. The English occupation, the devastation caused by the war and the economic crisis all had an effect on Paris. In 1348 the city was also struck by the Black Death that decimated the population.*

English grasp, a country girl, Joan of Arc, reached the French army and implored the Capetian King Charles VII, sheltering at Chinon, to allow her to march at the head of his troops. A miracle then took place. The enemy was routed and Charles VII entered Paris in triumph and was crowned as King. Joan of Arc was burnt to death, accused of witchcraft by the English, who eventually left French soil in 1453.

31 left *The English entered Paris in 1420 and upon the death of Charles VI proclaimed Henri VI of England King of France, even though he was still a child. However the indomitable, legendary figure of the Maid of Orléans soon appeared on the horizon. Here she is portrayed while fighting in front of the* Saint-Honoré gate. *It is said that she was sent by God to restore Charles VII, in hiding at Chinon to avoid the perils of the capital, to the throne of France. Thus Joan of Arc made her way to Chinon, where she arrived on March the 9th, 1429 to be presented to the King. When she found herself in front of the sovereign she said,* "My name is Joan, I have been sent by the King of the Heavens to tell you that you will be crowned as the true King of the French in the cathedral of Reims."

31 right *In this contemporary miniature, Charles VII is seated upon the French throne, surrounded by members of his court.*

In the fifteenth century, Paris, as Victor Hugo wrote, "was divided into three completely distinct and separate cities, each with its own shape, uniqueness, customs, traditions, privileges and history: the Cité, the Université and the Ville. Each of these three parts was a city, but a city too special to be complete and to be able to do without the other two. They therefore presented three individual faces. The Cité was a city of churches, the Ville of palaces, the Université of colleges... as if to say the island was the province of the bishop, the right bank of the merchants and the left bank of the rector". In the fifteenth century the Seine flowed around five islands, all

32 bottom The Valois line ended with Charles VIII, but it was through him that the Renaissance entered France. As shown in these engravings of the Abbey of Saint-Germain-des-Prés and the Louvre (left) and a palace under construction (right), Paris was already in a fervour of building, well-prepared to receive this new flowering of art.

*32 top
This contemporary painting shows Charles VIII, who succeeded his father, Louis XI, in 1483, under the regency of his sister Anna of Beaujeu. In 1491, at Langeais castle,*

he married the 15 year-old duchess Anna of Brittany, and at the urging of his advisors, in 1494 he travelled through Italy in order to annex Naples, enticed by the offers of exiles from the kingdom.

The expedition was immediately successful, but shortly thereafter, due to the strength of Naples' anti-French league, the King was forced to abandon the city and retreat back up the peninsula to France.

within the Paris city walls. Seen from above, each of these quarters appeared to be an inextricable tangle of twisting alleys from which the ornate Gothic architecture of many churches and palaces thrust its way into the sky.

Under Charles VIII and later Francis I, the great architectural and cultural phenomenon of the Italian Renaissance crossed the Alps and reached the banks of the Seine. Until then Paris had been a homogeneous city, an architectural and historical product of the Medieval. Now that severe unity was blended with the dazzling luxury of the new style, and softened by the introduction of rounded Romanesque arches, Greek columns and acanthus leaf volutes. The period saw the building of the Carnavalet, the Fountain of the Innocents, the Pont-Neuf and the Tuileries. In 1528 Francis I decided to move the court back to Paris following the intermission on the Loire, and to entrust Pierre Lescot with the complete rebuilding of the Louvre.

33 bottom left
This engraving shows Paris during the reign of Francis I. It was a city dominated by turrets and bell-towers that nevertheless reserved considerable space for greenery and nature, and boats rather than carts drawn by horses or oxen served the capital's commerce.

33 bottom right
In the 16th century Paris was a city of remarkable size, as this map dating back to the time of Francis I demonstrates.

33 top In 1528 Francis I, seen here dressed in damask, made his residence in Paris official. Besides expanding the Louvre, a project which he conferred upon the architect Lescot in 1546, the King began construction of a Hôtel de Ville worthy of his grandiose capital. Francis I, tall and anything but ugly, a fearless warrior, adored by his courtiers and loved by women, found a life-time adversary in Charles V, who had defeated him in the race for the Empire. The two sovereigns would have many opportunities to meet, but nothing positive that would bring peace to Europe was ever to come out of them. The ambitions of Francis I were in any case satisfied when, during a visit by Charles V to Paris, the city seemed, to the stupefied eyes of the Emperor, a city as large as the world.

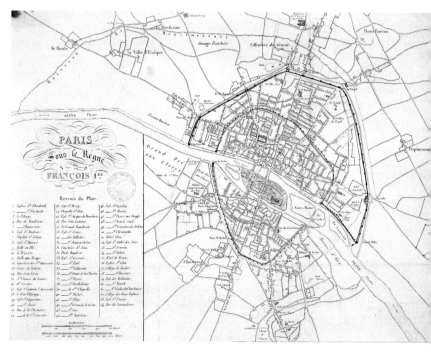

34 top Niece of Lorenzo the Magnificent, daughter of the Duke of Urbino Lorenzo de' Medici and the French Princess Madeleine d'Auvergne, and mother of three kings of France, Catherine de' Medici (in a painting depicting her when she was still young) had one of the most remarkable lives in history. In a century of both splendour and horror, she was educated in Florence, but at a very early age was sent to France to marry Henri of Orléans, the son of Francis I. The King never loved her, openly preferring throughout his life his lover Diana de Poitiers. However, Catherine, in spite of being despised as a foreigner and not of royal blood, was in a certain sense Queen for 30 years, as she was the mother of three Kings of France who succeeded one another. Her life was often in danger, but she confronted every risk with courage.

34-35 One of the finest qualities of Catherine de' Medici was her religious tolerance, but nevertheless, the massacre on the night of St. Bartholomew's Day happened during her reign on August 24th, 1572. This incident, in which thousands of Huguenots (French Protestants) were killed, is depicted here in a famous painting by François Dubois.

35 top right
This engraving
immortalises a difficult
moment for France on
the 12th of May, 1588,

when the capital was
barricaded and
violent clashes took
place over religious
differences.

*35 left This fresco
by Giorgio Vasari
in the Sala Regia
of the Vatican
portrays a scene of
the Saint
Bartholomew's Day
Massacre, in
particular its
justification by
Charles IX to the
Parliament.*

This was the era in which Rabelais, a Franciscan monk, attacked all and sundry from his priory near Tours, monks, the church, princes and politics feeling the weight of his pen. In the meantime Calvin was attracting proselytes for his Reformation. In Paris, the first to be infected by these new ideas were the wealthy merchants, the princes and the intellectuals. The Wars of Religion were not slow to break out, along with political in-fighting; In 1572 the

Huguenots were massacred in Paris on St. Bartholomew's Day permitted by Queen Catherine de' Medici. It was a difficult moment for France and the Huguenot King Henri IV who in order to enter Paris and save his throne was obliged to convert to Roman Catholicism, passing into history with the celebrated phrase "Paris is well worth a Mass" in 1594. Having assumed power he restored the city, causing it to rise from the ruins to the point where Paris represented the ideal city of an urban civilisation illuminated by the splendour of the King and his court. We are now at the threshold of the Grand Siècle: Descartes stirred debates among the intellectuals of the entire western world; the first great royal squares were completed: Place Dauphine and Place des Vosges.

*35 bottom right
In order to secure the
French crown, Henri
IV converted to
Catholicism. Once upon
the throne, he began a
restoration of the ruined
city, embellishing it with
new works, opening the
first large squares and
reviving work on
the Louvre and
the Tuileries. He also
inaugurated the Pont-
Neuf, encouraged the
development of the
Marais and the
urbanisation of the Ile
Saint-Louis. Moreover,
he had Place des Vosges
set out, initially as a
plaza for equestrian
competition, but high
aristocracy soon arrived
to live in the sumptuous
red brick buildings
surrounding the square.*

36 left   The King
of France and
Navarre, Louis XIII
(above), portrayed
in a famous
contemporary
painting, made Paris
a grand capital,
taking the initiative
on many projects,
but above all leaving
Cardinal Richelieu,
here depicted in his
official gowns, free
to construct the
Palais Cardinal,
today the Palais-
Royal.

36-37 and 36 bottom
By the 17th century
Paris had expanded
in all directions.
This map of the city
and the print dating

from that period
clearly demonstrate
this expansion and the
urban agglomeration
locked inside the city's
massive circular walls.

37 These engravings
show a number
of aspects of the
expanding city in
continuous growth.
Above one can
admire the
extraordinary view
of the Louvre and
the Seine from the
Pont-Neuf; the
painting in the centre
offers a view of the
Louvre, while the
painting below shows
the Seine as seen from
the Ile de la Cité.
In this period the
architect Louis Le
Barbier was creating
a new quarter on the
Rive Gauche between
the University and
the Seine, while
Christophe Marie was
constructing upon the
two little muddy and
uninhabited islands
bordering the Ile de
la Cité.

After the reign of Louis XIII (1610-1643), dominated by the controversial figure of the Prime Minister, Richelieu, the future Louis XIV (1643-1715) and the author of the famous phrase "I am the State", came to throne at just five years of age. He replaced the old city walls of Paris with great boulevards, promoted the creation of extensive public parks and built the grandiose Palace of Versailles to where, in 1682, the Sun King transferred his court.

The Sun King was succeeded by Louis XV (1715-1774), who also was to live at Versailles and was to devote himself to the embellishment of Paris, by now a city of around 500,000 inhabitants. He united the Faubourg Saint-Honoré with the Faubourg Saint-Germain with the Pont-Royal and had further bridges constructed over the Seine; he also ordered that the ancient cemetery of Saints-Innocents, a source of infection and disease, be demolished and replaced by a great market. In the meantime the Panthéon, the École Militaire and Place de la Concorde were all improved. On the international political front the disastrous Seven Years War (1756-1763) concluded with the loss of the colonies in Canada, the West Indies and India to the English, whilst the capital, in the absence of the King, was increasingly a hotbed of revolutionary ideas.

38 Whilst in 1500 Paris was experiencing a moment of glory and architectural reconstruction, it was also devastated by the Wars of Religion, aggravated by the Fronde activities that turned Louis XIV against the city (the Sun King is portrayed below alongside the drawings for the royal residence spread out on the table). It was under Louis XIV, in spite of his obsession with the dream of the Palace of Versailles, splendidly depicted above, that the city began to assume in part an appearance that we still recognise today. Sixty convents were built in the first decades of the 17th century. Largely thanks to Colbert, the controller of the finances and the superintendent of the monuments of the capital, during the reign of Louis XIV Paris saw the construction of many new buildings such as the Observatory and the Hôtel Royal des Invalides, designed by Hardouin-Mansart. This was the great architect and friend of the King who complied with and interpreted Louis XIV's desire to construct the immense Palace of Versailles.

39 top and bottom left Although absorbed by the Versailles project, Louis XV (portrayed below with the sceptre of power) did not forget Les Tuileries (above), to which continuous modifications were made. Great staircases, galleries and new apartments were built, whilst the garden, with its flower beds and fountains, where the noblemen and ladies would step aside as the King passed, became one of the most felicitous spaces of the grandiose construction.

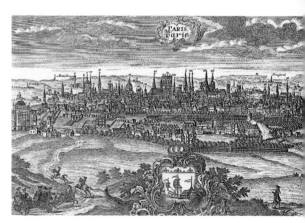

39 bottom right 17th-century Paris became ever more beautiful around Les Tuileries, as demonstrated by these images, which show a glimpse of the Seine and the cathedral of Notre-Dame (above) and a view of the port near the Tour Saint-Jacques (below).

40 left Historical events have made Louis XVI (portrayed above in his pompous coronation outfit) and Marie Antoinette of Austria, (at bottom, shown in a painting by Elisabeth-Louise Vigée-Lebrun), the most famous sovereigns in French history. She was the youngest and favourite of the 15 children of Emperor Frederick I and Maria Theresa of Austria. When she was only ten years old she was promised as the wife of the Dauphin of France, who was then only twelve.

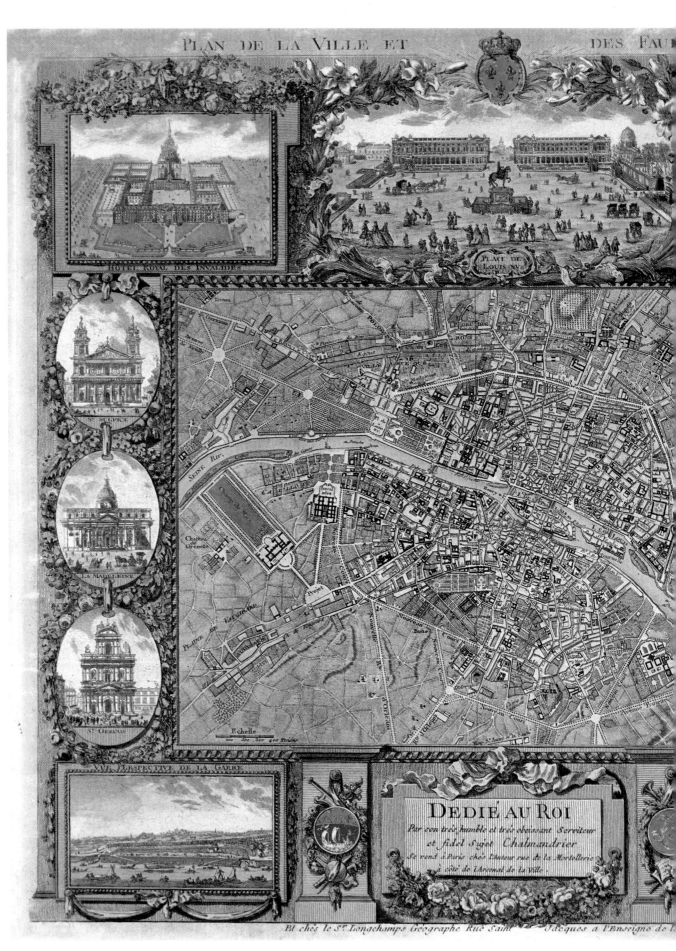

In an atmosphere that was by now hostile to the crown, Louis XVI came to the throne in 1774 with his Austrian wife Marie Antoinette. On the 5th of May, 1789, the States General met at Versailles in a climate of messianic expectation convinced that radical changes were on the horizon. Following the elaborate opening ceremony, and prior to tackling the real problems, the assembly was faced with a major procedural question over whether the motions presented should be voted according to order or per head. The representatives of the Third Estate (the upper and middles classes), numerically superior to the other two orders together (the nobility and the clerics), were in favour of voting per head whilst the others naturally preferred to vote per order as this would ensure them secure victory and confirm their privileges. The question seemed insoluble until the Third Estate suddenly proclaimed its own National Assembly in a surprising and highly significant move. Whilst the intervention of the King proved to be in vain, the privileged orders were obliged to bow to the will of the bourgeoisie and agree terms. On the 9th of July, 1789, the National Assembly was proclaimed as the Constituent Assembly and the States General ceased to exist. The King, however, still hoped to regain control of the situation by dismissing the liberal minister Necker and ordering a strong garrison to be placed around Versailles.

40-41 This map shows the development of Paris between 1785 and 1789.

41 While Marie Antoinette was squandering huge sums, the people were being infected by new revolutionary ideas. On the 5th of May, 1789, the States General met at Versailles (top) in a climate of expectation. Regardless of the fact that the atmosphere was perhaps not the most relaxed, a peaceful resolution to the conflicts was hoped for. However, the first signal of the Revolution had been sounded. The painting below shows the famous Jeu-de-Paume speech on the 20th of June, 1789.

This was the move that triggered the Revolution: on the 14th of July, 1789, the people, exasperated by a sharp rise in the price of bread and inflamed by revolutionary ideas, flooded the streets and squares and besieged the prison, the symbol of royal despotism. The storming of the Bastille had as an immediate consequence the constitution of a new municipal council the Commune, that immediately replaced the old aristocratic administrators with members of the bourgeoisie and decided upon the constitution of an urban militia, known as the National Guard, under La Fayette. A revolutionary wind blew throughout France. Following the Declaration of the Rights of Man the situation developed still further. On the 20th of June, 1791, Louis XVI escaped from the Tuileries where he had been obliged to reside after having left Versailles, and attempted to reach the troops faithful to him in Lorraine. However, after having been recognised at Varennes he was arrested and brought back under escort to Paris. Imprisoned in the Temple Tower, he was put on trial, condemned to death and executed on the 21st of January, 1793. The French Revolution, with all of the events and developments

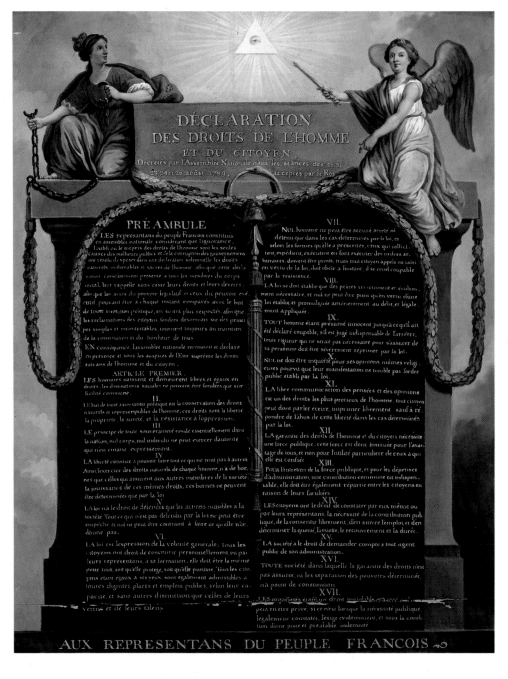

43 top left The protagonists of the Revolution inspired many artists. This image shows La Fayette at the Champs de Mars on the 14th of July, 1790.

43 bottom left The Musée Carnavalet contains many relics of the French Revolution, such as the symbol of the revolt as represented by the legendary phrase "Liberté Egalité."

43 top right Following the Revolution, the royal family left Versailles and returned to Paris. As prisoners of the Revolution they were held at Les Tuileries and later executed at the Place de la Concorde. In this painting Louis XVI is being accompanied to the gallows on the 21st of January, 1793.

43 bottom right Marat, the French revolutionary who in 1789 began publication of the newspaper L'Ami du peuple, is here being carried in triumph. His articles against the Assembly would have a significant impact upon the course of the revolution. He was one of the most active Montagnards (those who sat on the high benches in the Assembly) and president of the Jacobin club. In this capacity he conducted an open war against the Girondins. He was eventually assassinated by the knife of Charlotte Corday.

following the death of the King, had profound echoes throughout Europe. Goethe predicted as much upon the victory of the Jacobin volunteers over the Austrians and Prussians at Valmy on September 20th, 1792: "From this place and from this day begins a new era in the history of the world."

42 bottom
The Proclamation of the Rights of Man was heard as a new gospel that would lead to the liberation and regeneration of all men. The work of disciples of the philosophers, and apparently addressing all the populace, the Declaration of Rights clearly revealed its bourgeois origins, and was full of restrictions and conditions. Civil rights were conceded to all French citizens. Protestants and Jews were granted the right of citizenship, slavery was abolished in France but not in the colonies, and political rights were reserved for a minority.

After the Revolution, however, internal difficulties forced the country to seek new wars instead of peace. Early in 1796, the Directory planned a grand offensive against the Hapsburg. At the head of the army charged with restraining the Austrian troops in Italy while two other French units were attacking Austria from the German side, was Napoleon Bonaparte. A dark, bitter, and wild character, Napoleon Bonaparte had in him something of the haughtiness and rebelliousness of a Corsican bandit (he was born in Ajaccio in 1796), yet his military and political career was brilliant and unstoppable. Upon his return from the French campaign in Egypt he was appointed as the First Consul. In 1804, in the presence of the Pope, he crowned himself Emperor with his own hands at the cathedral of Notre-Dame. The setting was magnificent, worthy of a true royal coronation: he wore an embroidered gold tunic and was wrapped in an ermine-lined cloak decorated with golden bees. Four dignitaries were required to help him support this 40-kilogram costume. The famous Pitt diamond was set in the grip of his sword, while on his head was a precious crown of laurels glittering with diamonds — the work of Biennais, the court jeweller, and costing eight thousand francs. This grandiose moment also signalled the beginning of the legend of the great Corsican: the Emperor declared war against half of Europe, defeated the Austrians at Austerlitz, descended into Italy, and then confronted the terrible Russian winter with the dream of deposing the Czar, but failed. Napoleon's epic invasion ended in catastrophe. In March, 1814 the allies conquered Paris: Russians, Prussians, Cossacks and Austrians marched down the Champs-Élysées. Napoleon abdicated and left for the island of Elba. The Congress of Vienna consigned the throne of France to the Bourbons, but in March 1815 Napoleon escaped from Elba, landed in the south of France and marched upon Paris. His "100 days" finished at Waterloo: he was defeated by the English, and then exiled to the remote island of St. Helena in the middle of the Atlantic Ocean, where he died in 1821.

45 These images present two episodes of Napoleon's military campaign with the Russian troops encamped upon the Champs Élysées on the 31st of March, 1814 (top), and the entry of the allied powers into Paris (bottom).

46 top The Revolution left Paris with no significant monuments apart from the grand patriotic space of the Champs de Mars. Sacking and confiscations took place in this period, and vast estates belonging to religious orders or members of the aristocracy were liberated and passed into the hands of new speculators. The Commission of Artists was formed to give new order to the city plan, but with no great results. Napoleon was even more brutal and when he became First Consul he affirmed that "if Paris is to be beautified there is more to demolish than to construct. Why not knock down the whole quarter of the Cité, that vast ruin fit to house only rats?" As Emperor he could realise his dream of making Paris the most beautiful city in the world. He opened Rue Rivoli, and had the market of Les Halles reorganised. Four bridges were built across the Seine, the arch on the Carrousel was constructed and the colossal Arc de Triomphe on the Étoile was begun. The Palais du Luxembourg, seen here, became the home to the Senate under Napoleon.

46 centre and bottom Napoleon's grand innovative and revivalist plans for the rebirth of Paris also included the completion of the construction of La Madeleine, centre, that resembles a Greek temple. Napoleon housed his veteran soldiers at the Hôtel des Invalides (bottom).

46

46-47 The Panthéon, seen here in a famous painting depicting it in the mid-19th century, houses the tombs of the most illustrious figures of France.

47 top These two illustrations present two celebrated Paris churches. Saint-Sulpice (left), which after Notre-Dame is the largest church in Paris, and Saint-Etienne-du-Mont (right), a singular church in which the Gothic styling is already showing signs of the innovative new wind of the Renaissance.

48 top Under Louis
XVIII, portrayed
here in his sumptuous
coronation gowns
(left), and during a
party given in his
honour at the Odéon
theatre in 1819
(right), nobody was
concerned with
changing or
enriching the face of
Paris.

48-49 At the behest
of Napoleon and in
honour of the victory
of the Grande Armée,
a column based on
Trajan's column
drawn from Rome
was erected in the
Place Vendôme. Cast
from the bronze of
melted cannons taken
from the enemies at
Austerlitz, the
column is a
continuous spiral of
historical bas-reliefs.

49 top left Like his
predecessor Louis
XVIII, Charles X
did little in the way of
providing Paris with
new architectural
works.

49 top right
The construction
of the Arc de
Triomphe, begun by
Napoleon Bonaparte
in 1806, was completed
during the reign
of Charles X.

49 bottom right
On 25th of October,
1836, a great obelisk
from Luxor was
erected in Place de la
Concorde as this
contemporary print
illustrates.

The Revolution had sacked and confiscated, but had not built any great monuments except for the patriotic expanse of the Champs-de-Mars parade ground, the stage for national celebrations and military exercises. After the sober, precious Louis XVI style, and the Neo-classicism of the Directory with its richer architectural features, the glory of Napoleon Bonaparte came to be celebrated in the first decades of the nineteenth century in monumental works. The marble Arc de Triomphe was erected at the end of the Champs Élysées, the Rue de Rivoli was relaid and at the centre of the Place Vendôme a column cast in bronze from enemy cannons captured at Austerlitz was inaugurated on August 15th, 1810. A symbol of the glorious Napoleonic era, it was decorated with a bas-relief depicting the feats of the Grand Armée.

The nineteenth century advanced with political instability under the new rulers Louis XVIII (1815-1824), and his successor Charles X. The Romantics, with their long hair, red vests, and flowing shirts, challenged the conservatives with the dreams of liberty brought forth in their work.

The heroic symbol of this period was *Hernani* by Victor Hugo, which opened one memorable evening on the stage of the Théâtre Français.

50 top and 50-51 Baron Haussmann, portrayed below whilst receiving from Napoleon III the decree annexing the suburban communes to Paris, was responsible for the conception of the 19th-century city. Gutting and levelling whole quarters, building others from scratch, laying out very broad streets to meet the new demands of urban traffic, within a few years he imposed upon medieval, baroque, romantic Paris a new modern, imperial vision of the capital, the plan of which can be seen reproduced above.

51 top This painting embellished with pretty cherubs depicts the monumental Louvre complex at the time of Napoleon III, himself portrayed in the frieze at the top.

51 bottom and centre The demolition of Paris by Haussmann provoked great controversy at the time. In 1859 the poet Charles Baudelaire wrote, "The old Paris is no more". In these photos you can see two buildings erected during this period: the Opéra Garnier (top), considered a model of the Baroque style that characterised the reign of Napoleon III and the central market Les Halles (bottom), built between 1852 and 1859.

In February, 1848, the Second Republic was proclaimed (the first having had a short life during the Revolution of 1792), with the unanimous election of Louis Napoleon Bonaparte as its leader. Four years later he would assume the title of Emperor of the French with the name Napoleon III. The Second Empire, which concluded in 1870, was a period of relative liberalism: the field of art saw the explosion of Impressionism; literature flourished with works of protest and rebellion; while Paris itself was subjected to the daring urban transformations of Baron Georges Haussman, who for 40 years left Parisians to walk through the mud of construction sites that were to provide the city with the most beautiful streets in the world. However, the city suffered serious damage during the disasterous Franco-Prussian war and in the subsequent months when the French regular army besieged the capital in a cruel attempt to put down the insurrection that broke out following the surrender.

52 With a series of state interventions Napoleon attempted to meet the demands of a country in the process of transformation. This was the period in which roads, canals and railway networks expanded and the great avenues, squares and sumptuous buildings were created. Napoleon III's policy was designed to revive the spirit of revolutionary France, but the war of 1870 consumed this euphoria and laid the basis for the fall of the imperial regime.

The revolt exploded in Paris on 18th of March, 1871: the Commune was constituted as a revolutionary government. The illustrations on this page depict the salient events of those days: at the top, the revolutionaries and the manifesto of the Commune; in the centre, the assembled representatives of the Commune; bottom, the disturbances in the capital.

The Third Republic came about following the violent struggles between the National Assembly (still controlled by the monarchy) and the revolutionary government, known as the Commune, installed in Paris on March 18th, 1871. In just a few short weeks, this new revolutionary regime succeeded in demonstrating the validity of applied socialism, an event which later would serve as an exemplar for Karl Marx. The restoration of peace coincided with the birth of Impressionism, the art movement led by Monet, Renoir, Pissarro, Cézanne and Manet. The first exhibition was held in the studio of the photographer Nadar, but it was not until 1877 that the term *Impressionistes* was officially acknowledged.

53 top and centre These two contemporary illustrations depict a sad moment in the history of Paris: the Prussians besieged and bombarded the capital at the end of the terrible Franco-Prussian war.

53 bottom After the fall of the Empire, the Third Republic was proclaimed and this contemporary print illustrates the general euphoria the event provoked.

54 top left and centre left The Belle Époque was a period of frenetic creativity: Art Nouveau was all the rage — the work of A. Mucha (top left) was a clear synthesis of the airy canons of the style — and an evening at the Folies-Bergère was not to be missed (centre left).

54 centre right This unusual photo has captured a moment in the construction of the celebrated Statue of Liberty, presented to the United States by France.

At the end of the century, Paris blossomed in the fields of art, music and the theatre. Paris became the stage for the birth of modernity: the *Belle Époque* dawned, Art Nouveau burst onto the scene, the first Metro lines were laid and gas lighting was adopted. The unmistakable outline of the Eiffel Tower climbed into the sky. In the first decade of the new century, Braque and Picasso overturned the old artistic canons with Cubism, inagurating an extraordinary period of creativity that was to see artists such as Fernand Léger and Marcel Duchamp. All of Europe was however heading towards one of the most tragic periods of its history.

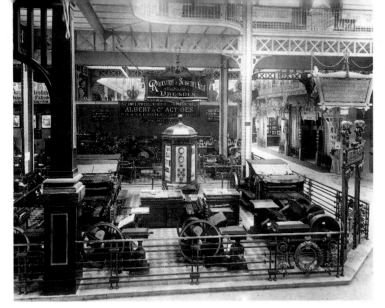

54 bottom This photo shows a typical Paris Metro station. Work on the system under the direction of Fulgence Bienvenue began late in 1898. The road entrances were conceived in the style of the age, 141 of them being designed by Hector Guimard, father of French Art Nouveau.

54-55 The 1889 World's Fair in Paris, of which here we can see the main entrance (bottom) and an exhibition hall (top right), had as its dominating symbol the Eiffel Tower (top left), designed by the French engineer from whom it takes its name. As it climbed into the capital's sky, the celebrated Iron Lady aroused fierce controversy with its detractors signing petitions of disgust and condemnation of the bizarre construction. Many intellectuals entered the debate, claiming that the beauty of Paris would be ruined by that "ugly factory chimney".

During the First World War the city was saved from an invasion of the German troops, but in the course of the second conflict the German army marched beneath the Arc de Triomphe. The city folded in on itself.

Following the capitulation, General Charles De Gaulle launched an appeal from the studios of the BBC asking the French people to continue the resistance against the Germans. Finally, the allies landed in Normandy and Nazi Germany was defeated.

The Fourth Republic saw a series of unstable governments that hindered economic recovery. The war in Indochina concluded in defeat for France, while on the horizon loomed the dramatic prospect of war with Algeria. The Fifth Republic was born in 1958 with the election of General De Gaulle as President, brought back to power in order to avoid a coup d'état. This relaunched France on the international scene. In 1962 De Gaulle signed the Evian Accords, which put an end to the war in Algeria.

In the now legendary May of 1968, the claims of students and workers were heard on barricaded squares, signalling a significant moment in the city's history. Once order had been restored, a number of concessions were made, including a reform of the education system. In the presidential elections of 1969, De Gaulle was overtaken by Georges Pompidou, who was in turn succeeded by Valéry Giscard d'Estaing in 1974, and François Mitterrand in 1981. Leader of the socialist party, Mitterrand was re-elected for a second term, but was then defeated by Jacques Chirac in the elections of 1995. These last Presidents were also the moving spirits behind new developments affecting Paris's urban future. Pompidou bequeathed his name to the bizarre Beaubourg, "the blue refinery," as it was defined by its detractors. Giscard d'Estaing approved the plans for the Musée d'Orsay, the Cité des Sciences et des Tecniques at La Villette, and the Institut du Monde Arabe. However, the most ambitious projects were those of François Mitterrand: the Grand Louvre, the Arche de la Défense, the Opéra-Bastille and the Grande Bibliotèque, built "to preserve the historical memory of France", and, above all, in order to surprise the world and exalt once again the eternal *grandeur* of the *Ville Lumière*.

58 top and 59 top
The Ile de la Cité is
the cradle of ancient
Lutetia, *the historic
heart of the city.
The island contains
not only remains
of the Roman*
oppidum *and some
of the city's most
important
monuments such
as Notre-Dame and
Sainte Chapelle,
but also two of
the most romantic
and exclusive corners:
the Square Galant
and the intimate
Place Dauphine,
constructed at the
behest of Henri IV
to the design approved
by Sully, in honour
of the Dauphin of
France, the future
Louis XIII.*

*58-59 The Seine
and the Eiffel Tower
are two symbols of
the Ville Lumière.
In spite of being
defined as an old
factory chimney by
its detractors, the
celebrated tower
continues to be one
of the capital's most
popular monuments.
Work began on the
tower in January,
1887 and was
completed two years,
two months and five
days later, just in
time for the
inauguration of the
World's Fair of 1889
of which it was
intended to be
the symbol.*

59 right The Ile Saint-Louis, whilst linked to the Ile de la Cité, is a world apart, isolated and deaf to the noise and bustle that surround it. Thanks to this exclusiveness the island has always been inhabited by celebrities such as Georges Pompidou who had a home on Quai de Béthune, Baron Guy de Rothschild and the actress Michèle Morgan. In the 14th century, the island served only as pasture for livestock. In the 17th century the land was reclaimed and divided into lots. The streets that now criss-cross the island are lined with beautiful 17-century buildings, a number of exclusive boutiques and small bistros.

Paris was born on two small islands in the Seine: a world apart from the rest of the city, a world containing some of the capital's most significant monuments. Here on the Ile de la Cité are the roots of Celtic *Lutetia*, a village founded by a group of fisherman of the Parisii tribe in 200 B.C. The Ile Saint-Louis seems to have been frozen in the Grand Siècle, a era of elegant houses and silent streets, an oasis of peace and austere aristocracy. Crossing the Pont-Neuf, the oldest bridge in Paris, initiated by Henri III late in the sixteenth century and opened by Henri IV in 1607 (the nineteenth-century statue depicting him mounted on his horse separates the tip of the island from the Place Dauphine) you enter the living political and religious history of Paris.

*60 top left
The southern facade
of the Palais de
Justice faces onto
the Quai des Orfèvres
where in the 12th
and 13th centuries
craft workshops and
jewellers flourished.
This photo shows the
main entrance to
the Palais de Justice,
separated from the
street by an imposing
Louis XVI-style
18th-century gate.*

*60 bottom left In the
Conciergerie, the
state prison during
the Reign of Terror,
are to be found the
Salle des Pas-Perdus
and the Chambre
Dorée where in 1793
the sittings of the
Revolutionary
Tribunal led to
the summary trials
that sent guilty
and innocent victims
alike to the guillotine.*

*60 top right
More recently the
celebrated writer
Georges Simenon
identified the Palais
de Justice with the
imaginary "PJ",
the legendary French
judicial police
of the detective
Maigret.*

*60-61 and 61 top
Sainte-Chapelle,
a jewel of Gothic art,
exalts the mysticism
of an epoch with its
airy, soaring
structure and the
multi-coloured
transparencies of its
windows, as these
photos show.*

The Palais de Justice features the city's oldest public clock, one which has struck the hours for six centuries thanks to the precision mechanism designed by the German watchmaker Henri Vic in 1370. This building became the seat of the Paris Parliament when Charles V shifted the royal residence to the Louvre and afterwards became the Palais de Justice during the French Revolution. The stark walls of the Conciergerie and the adjoining, sinister prison still evoke the tragic moments when those condemned to death during the Terror left from here, in long white shirts, to be guillotined in Place de la Concorde. From the turbulent years of the Revolution to the mysticism of La Sainte-Chapelle. The precious chapel enclosed within the walls of the Palais de Justice is a masterpiece of Gothic art, built at the beginning of the thirteenth century at the behest of the sainted Louis IX, King of France, to house priceless relics of the Crown of Thorns and the Holy Cross from Byzantium. It boasts large stained glass windows that leave almost no room for the stonework: these windows are a triumph of bright red and blue and narrate scenes from Genesis, the Old Testament, and the life of Christ.

62 *This photo shows the beautiful west facade of the cathedral of Notre-Dame with the three-part vertical structure accentuated by the portals. Restoration work on Notre-Dame was begun in 1845 and completed in 1864 by the architect Eugène Emmanuel Viollet-le-Duc.*

The most precious monument of the Ile de la Cité is the Cathedral of Notre-Dame, towering and immense on the Place du Parvis-Notre-Dame, a clearing created by Haussmann at the time of Napoleon III to exalt the building's celebrated facade and that conceals the vestiges of the primitive Gallic *Lutetia.* "Every wall, every stone of this venerable monument is a page not only from the history of France," wrote Victor Hugo, "but also of science and art. Among all the old churches of Paris, this central, mother-church is a kind of chimera: it has the head of this, the limbs of that, and the torso of another, something from everything. Each flux of time has brought its own alluvial deposit, every race has made its own contribution to the monument, each individual has added a stone. Like great mountains, great buildings are also the works of centuries." In 1163 Bishop Maurice de Sully invited Pope Alexander III himself to lay the foundation stone of the cathedral, during the reign of Louis VIII. Thus on the foundations of the primitive church of St. Stephen, a new basilica was erected, reflecting that anxiety over the infinite that animated the consciences of men of the thirteenth century. The construction of Notre-Dame lasted roughly two hundred years and finished midway through the fourteenth century. All the history of France has passed through these imposing naves, including the French Revolution which "consecrated" the Cathedral to the cult of the God of Reason, plundering and sullying it in the process. A walk around the outside of Notre-Dame reveals the masterful interplay of architectural elements: rampant arches, spires, peaks, windows, doors, rose-windows, and a magical population of monsters and demons emerging from magnificent doorways or springing out from pilasters garlanded with acanthus. The view from the top of the tower of Notre-Dame is a panorama of light and air over all of Paris and the nearby Ile Saint-Louis. Linked to the Ile de la Cité by the Pont Saint-Louis, this island is quiet and relatively undisturbed by tourism, a tongue of land laid gently down in the Seine, and the residence of many of the capital's leading figures. This island features a succession of old seventeenth-century patrician residences such as the Hôtel de Lauzun, which housed the poet Charles Baudelaire and the bohemian artistic and literary circles of his time.

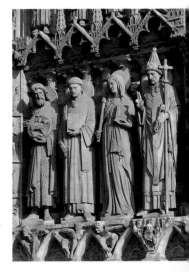

63 *top left
The Gallery of the Kings, only part of which can be seen here, contains 19th-century copies of 28 statues of the French Kings; the originals were destroyed during the Revolution.*

63 *bottom left
In front of the western rose-window can be seen the Virgin Mary and to either side representations of the virtues and vices.*

63 *right The portals of Notre-Dame are heavily decorated with fine sculptures. In this photo you can see two details of the Door of the Virgin, the sculptures for which were executed in the 13th century.*

64-65 The flourishing of the Gothic style in France between the 11th and the 15th centuries can be seen in many cathedrals from the era throughout the country. Among the most famous of these is undoubtedly the cathedral of Notre-Dame, the most venerated Parisian church, begun in 1163 at the behest of St. Louis IX and completed over the next 150 years. In its grandiosity it was intended to rival the nearby Saint-Denis. The cathedral earned literary immortality in the famous novel by Victor Hugo as the setting for the unhappy stories of Esmeralda

and Quasimodo, and under its roof a number of significant chapters in the history of France have been written. Here Mary Stuart was married, Joan of Arc was proclaimed a saint, Abelard met Heloïse, Henri VI of England was crowned as the child King of France, Napoleon crowned himself Emperor of the French in 1804 and in 1944 General De Gaulle announced the end of the German occupation of Paris. The cathedral was devastated and stripped of its treasures during the French Revolution. In the autumn of 1793 the vandals destroyed many of the statues and the building was consecrated to the God of Reason. Only in 1795 was Notre-Dame reconsigned to the Church, purified and in 1802 once again held Catholic services. Through a small door close to the north tower you can climb to the top of the cathedral to enjoy the stunning panorama.

The Petit-Pont is Paris's shortest bridge and at one time everyone, save the usual fraudsters, paid a toll to cross it. At the far end of the bridge from the Ile de la Cité lies the legendary Left Bank, a community of churches and convents before becoming famous for its bars and bistros, Saint-Germain and the Latin Quarter. Above the mansard roofs of the imposing mansions rise the curves of historic domes. Some are sublime, such as that covering the Institut de France. This is the most beautiful

dome in the country, standing over the building in which the five National Academies meet in plenary assembly each October. Some are noble, such as that of the Hôpital du Val de Grâce, built in the sixteenth century to thank God for having provided France with an heir to the Crown, the future Louis XIV. Some domes are imposing, such as that of the Panthéon in the Latin Quarter, a tribute to the nation's heroes. Since 1791 many illustrious figures, intellectuals and famous literati such as Mirabeau, Voltaire, Rousseau, Marat, Victor Hugo and Emile Zola have been laid to rest below the vaults of this solemn building (which is based upon a Greek cross plan). Marie Curie, who died in 1934, is the only woman to be included in this celebrated company. From the top of the dome hangs the famous Foucault's Pendulum (perhaps to be relocated once again), which in 1851 was used by the celebrated French physicist to demonstrate the rotation of the planet. The "dome of knowledge" is that of the Sorbonne, the celebrated Parisian university founded by Robert de Sorbon, a rector and confidant of the king. In 1528 de Sorbon obtained the authorization to found the Collège de Sorbon for poor students and teachers desiring to further their studies in theology. To aid the realization of a *Universitas Studiorum*, Louis IX and Cardinal Richelieu (who is buried at the Sorbonne in a marble coffin) ordered the construction of a new building by the architect Le Mercier, of which only the chapel remains today. Between 1885 and 1901 the entire complex was rebuilt, and today it occupies a vast portion of the Latin Quarter. Just a step away are the Luxembourg Gardens: "there is nothing more charming," wrote Léon Daudet, "nor anything more inviting of idleness and daydream, or to young lovers, who, on sweet spring mornings or beautiful summer evenings, slip into the shadows of hundred-year old trees."

66-67 and 67 top right The Panthéon, "the enforced gift of the Church and the Kings to the Republic" as it has been defined, stands on the Sainte-Geneviève hill and houses the tombs of some of France's most illustrious figures. The facade was inspired by ancient Greek architecture and the magnificent dome rises proudly above it.

67 top left This photo shows the superb 17th-century architecture of the Institut de France, a building financed by Mazarin and designed by Louis le Vau.
In the east wing of the building is the library dedicated to the distinguished statesman and housing precious volumes.

*68 Historic figures
such as Diderot,
Beaudelaire and
Alfred de Musset
have enjoyed strolling
along the avenues
of the Luxembourg
Gardens. The latter
defined the gardens
as "a delightful place,*

*a solitary haven
open day and night
for the student with
his books under his
arm, for the dreamer
and his indolence
and for the lover with
his beloved who meet
here as if in
Paradise".*

*68-69 The Luxembourg
Gardens officially
belong to the Senate as
they surround the
grandiose building of
the same name in which
the senators assemble. In
reality however they are
the refuge of the students
from the nearby
universities and all
those looking for
peace and tranquility
amidst their luxuriant
greenery.*

*69 top The Luxembourg
Gardens were created
in 1617 by Boyeau de
la Bareaudière, the
first authority on
French-style gardens.
The numerous statues
set along the avenues
were mostly erected
during the reign of
Louis Philippe in the
19th century.*

The Luxembourg Gardens encircle the Palais du Luxembourg (today occupied by the senate of the Republic of France), the Florentine island constructed to remind Maria de' Medici of the Palazzo Pitti in Florence. At all hours of the day students stop to rest on the terraces of the bars or in the windows of the bistros in the Latin Quarter, so named because in medieval times the official language used by professors and students was Latin, and also because this community — bounded by the Luxembourg Gardens, the Seine, and the Boulevard St-Michel — is built upon the ancient plan of the Gallic *Lutetia*. Not far from here, in fact, the shadow of Caesar is still cast on the Arènes de Lutèce, an amphitheatre probably constructed sometime in the first century AD, the heart of ancient *Lutetia* and unearthed in 1869 during an excavation of the Rue Monge, and on the Cluny Baths, where, amidst green fields and thick forests, the Romans would relax at the end of a fatiguing day.

The Musée National du Moyen-Age and the Cluny Baths contain the remains of three large rooms: the *frigidarium*, the *tepidarium*, and the *calidarium*. Backing onto the baths and built late in the fifteenth century is the Hôtel des Abbés de Cluny, itself the custodian of a collection of rare masterpieces of medieval art, including the six tapestries based upon the theme of the "Dame à la licorne", masterpieces of Flemish textile art.

The Left Bank is also rich in famous churches: Saint-Severin in the Flemish Gothic style, "delicate and small in a poor corner of Paris," is how the writer Huysmans described it, where it's said that even Dante came to pray during his supposed trip to Paris; Saint-Julien-le-Pauvre, in the heart of the university life of the city, encircled by the tight alleys of a most picturesque Paris (near the church, at Place Viviani, there is a curiosity: here grows the oldest tree in Paris, a false acacia or Robinia, planted in 1601 by the botanist J. Robin, from whom the species takes its name); Saint-Etienne-du-Mont, just a stone's throw away from the Panthéon, noted for the decoration of its splendid Renaissance *jubé* as well as for the remains of St. Geneviève, the patron saint of Paris, buried here today in a chapel not far from those of Pascale and Racine. Finally, of course, the most famous of all the churches of Paris and also the oldest: Saint-Germain-des-Prés, the abbey founded in 543 by King Childebert in the open countryside, of the vast plain where the Parisii were defeated by the Roman legionnaires. The interior features three naves, beautiful capitals on the choir stalls and frescoed walls, and up high, the sharp spires of a Romanesque bell-tower preside over one of the liveliest squares on the Left Bank, not far from Saint-Sulpice, the largest church in Paris after Notre-Dame. At the end of the Boulevard St. Germain, along the Quai Saint-Bernard, sparkles the curved facade of the Institute du Monde Arabe, built in 1987 by the architect Jean Nouvel: ten stories upon which aluminium diaphragms, inspired by the Alhambra of Granada, open and close according to the light of the sun, in a continuous dialogue between Arab architecture and modern technology. Beyond this is an oasis of peace: the Jardin des Plantes, the grandiose botanical gardens surrounding the Musée National d'Histoire Naturelle. This was a royal garden of medicinal herbs during the reign of Louis XIII, and was opened to the public in 1640. A modern restoration commissioned by Mitterrand sits happily with the metalwork of the Galerie de l'Évolution leaving intact the exciting view of the long rows of stuffed giraffes, rhinoceroses, hippopotamuses, zebras, antelope, and elephants that seem to go on forever. From Saint-Germain-des-Prés, the Rue de Rennes meets Montparnasse and its most striking symbol: the Tour Montparnasse, a giant steel and glass structure that has been piercing the sky since 1973. The tower is 210 metres tall, with 59 storeys that are climbed in an instant in an incredibly fast elevator, and it commands a breathtaking view of Paris. From here it may seem almost impossible to tie the threads of this small hill's past and the myths woven around it by Apollinaire and the artists who at the beginning of the twentieth century elected the area the "navel of the world," to the current urban agglomeration and the busy swarming of the populace at its feet. There remains the Musée Bourdelle on the Rue Antoine-Bourdelle to evoke something of the spirit that animated Montparnasse at the beginning of the twentieth century. The studio of the celebrated sculptor, and favourite pupil of Rodin, houses more than five hundred works of art that were created within its walls between 1884 and 1929, the year of the artist's death.

70-71 In the twilight Paris is illuminated like some fantastic stage set. Out of the shadows emerge the most distinguished monuments, cars trace bands of light along the grand boulevards, Rue de Rennes being seen here, and the city unfurls its joie de vivre *in anticipation of the adventures of the night to come. This photo shows the floodlit facades of the most celebrated churches of the Rive Gauche, Saint-Germain-des-Prés on the left and Saint-Sulpice on the right.*

72-73 Against the backdrop of the stunning panorama to be seen from the top of the Eiffel Tower stands the imposing Tour Montparnasse, a steel and concrete building constructed in 1973.

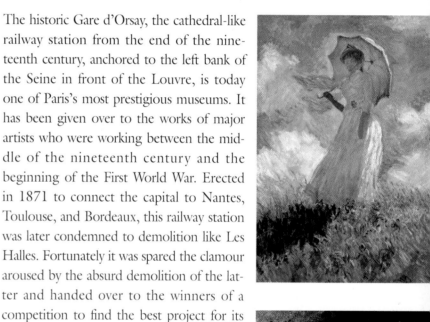

The historic Gare d'Orsay, the cathedral-like railway station from the end of the nineteenth century, anchored to the left bank of the Seine in front of the Louvre, is today one of Paris's most prestigious museums. It has been given over to the works of major artists who were working between the middle of the nineteenth century and the beginning of the First World War. Erected in 1871 to connect the capital to Nantes, Toulouse, and Bordeaux, this railway station was later condemned to demolition like Les Halles. Fortunately it was spared the clamour aroused by the absurd demolition of the latter and handed over to the winners of a competition to find the best project for its revival. This huge building, made of iron and stone from Buxi, was converted into the Musée d'Orsay by the Italian architect Gae Aulenti in 1986 and is now one of the largest and most visited museums of the capital. The immense central nave, where the steam locomotives used to belch smoke, has been transformed into a labyrinth of clear light and suspended walls like theatre backdrops, which leave visitors free to wander, rather than imposing a particular path. The museum has assembled the works of many of the most fascinating artists of the nineteenth century: Ingres and Delacroix; the acclaimed Impressionists once housed in the old Jeu de Paume museum: Degas, Monet, Manet, Pissarro, Renoir, Cézanne, Van Gogh, Gauguin, Seurat, Toulouse-Lautrec, and Matisse; the realists Daumier, Millet, Corot, and Courbet; academy painters; the furniture of Gallé; and the works of Camille Claudel.

77 top Camille Pissarro, 1830-1903, succeeded in bringing to the canvas the magical, mysterious atmosphere of Paris, as in this painting entitled La Seine et Le Louvre.

77 centre left This extremely well known 1889 painting by Van Gogh, La Chambre de Van Gogh en Arles, *reveals all the strength and* the bold handling of paint typical of the great Dutch artist.

77 centre right Paul Gauguin, 1848-1903, was initially an Impressionist painter, but subsequently developed a very personal pictorial style. Here we can admire his 1892 painting Joyeusetés.

77 bottom left Edgar Degas successfully captured the grace and lightness of a group of classical ballerinas waiting to perform in his Danseuses bleues *of 1893.*

77 bottom right Henri de Toulouse-Lautrec immortalised La Clownesss Cha-u-Kao du Moulin Rouge *in 1895.*

76 When Napoleon III came to power in 1852 there was an explosion in of creativity in all fields of life and the arts. Poets flourished and painters began to pay a greater attention to reality, giving rise to the successful period of Realism and Impressionism. Other celebrated works conserved in the Musée d'Orsay were created in these fertile years, including this work by Van Gogh depicting L'église d'Auverse-sur-Oise executed in 1890.

78 top and 78-79
Napoleonic
monumental Paris
is represented by
the École Militaire
(top right) and
the broad expanse
of the Champs de
Mars across which

echo memories of the
Grande Armée.
Below the imposing
gilded cupola of
the Dôme (bottom)
lie the remains of
Napoleon in a
porphyry sarcophagus
(top left).

And here we are in monumental Paris, dominated by the golden cupola of the Dôme, under which Napoleon rests. In this Paris of grand spaces, long views, and the sumptuous noble and bourgeois mansions of the nobility, the city celebrates its eternal *grandeur*. From the Champs-de-Mars to the École Militaire, the country's foremost military academy, military memories echo across the broad parade ground that could at one time accommodate ten thousand mounted troops and pervade the still atmosphere of the Musée de l'Armée, with its rich collections of weapons of all eras, swords, pistols, firearms, crossbows, muskets, armour, maps and plans, flags and banners embroidered by hand with various coats of arms. The Hôtel des Invalides, commissioned by Louis XIV for housing injured, ill, or elderly, retired soldiers, features a golden dome containing the porphyry tomb of Napoleon according to the last wishes of the great leader: "I would like my ashes laid to rest on the banks of the Seine, in the midst of the people of France, whom I have loved so much." A few steps away from the Dôme is the Musée Rodin, dedicated to the genius who still seduces us today, the artist who between the 19th and the 20th centuries filled the international scene with his celebrated sculptures, the eclectic romantic who opened the door to modernity for all of his contemporaries. At the beginning of the century, on the advice of his friend Rainer Maria Rilke, he established his studio-museum in the *rocaille* setting of the Hôtel Biron, a temple of bronze monuments and famous works like the *La Main de Dieu* and the celebrated *Kiss*.

79 Close to Les Invalides, at the end of Rue de Varenne, is the Musée Rodin, housed in the beautiful rooms of the Hôtel Biron. The photos show the entrance to the museum (top), a room dedicated to one of the sculptor's most famous works, the celebrated Kiss (centre) and lastly one of the master's works exhibited in the garden overlooked by the museum that stands out against the grandiose backdrop of the gilded dome over Napoleon's tomb (bottom).

It is now only a step to the celebrated Eiffel Tower. 7,300 tonnes of iron went into the construction of this "ridiculous factory fireplace," "the gigantic skewer, good for poking the clouds" (as it was described at the time it was built), a grey structure rising wildly from its solid foundations on the Champ-de-Mars. On 12th of June, 1886, the engineer Gustave Eiffel won the city of Paris's competition: the World's Fair of 1889 chose this "grande dame of iron" as its symbol from amongst 107 proposals. The workers began construction at the

feet, the Pont d'Iéna crosses over the Seine and arrives at the hill of Chaillot, high against the right bank of the river and home to the semicircular Palais de Chaillot, constructed for the 1937 Paris exhibition. The building contains the Musée de la Marine, which will take you to the high seas, the Musée de l'Homme, with its history of the world in reverse, and the Musée du Cinema Henri Langlois, where the ghosts of Rudolph Valentino, Marilyn Monroe, Greta Garbo, and Federico Fellini are brought back to life.

80-81 The Eiffel Tower was from the very outset a "monster" that could be seen from all four corners of Paris as it soared high above all the city's greatest monuments. Today the bizarre construction, the fruit of laborious calculations, is no longed regarded with desecrating irony, but rather as the most acrobatic and glorious symbol of the city.

It required a gestation period of two years during which time it grew to a height of 276 metres, the antenna topping out at 318 metres. The 18,030 cast iron sections and two and a half million rivets weigh a total of 10,000 tonnes. Should you wish to climb to the top on foot then 1,665 steps await you.

beginning of July, 1887, and soon all heads were turning upwards to stare at the marvel of the century — such a strange, crude construction that day by day climbed higher towards the sky like some crazed, gangly giant who had taken the era's claim that progress was made of metal much too literally. The official inauguration was held in May, 1889. Since then, six million visitors per year (one hundred and sixty million in total!) have climbed to the top to take in the breathtaking expanse of Paris. At the Tower's

Great flights of steps run down the sides of the hill, and intrepid youths execute crazy skateboard stunts in the square. We are still in the Paris of grand spaces and long views that lead to the Étoile and to that colossal symbol of the city, the Arc de Triomphe, a solemn anthem to glorious victory. Upon his return from the Battle of Austerlitz in 1806, Napoleon commissioned this immense and pharaonic monument to celebrate his men's triumphant military campaign. The view in one direction from the top of the arch takes in the major artery that leads to the Grande Arche de la Défense, Otto von Spreckelsen's cube covered in white Carrara marble and inaugurated in the bicentenary of the French Revolution. In the other direction the Champs-Élyseés leads to the Place de la Concorde, and Les Tuileries. A military parade marches down this street every July 14th, with much fanfare and fluttering of tricolour flags. This old vie Royale was initially laid out only up to the Étoile, in order to extend the Les Tuileries gardens and to create a grandiose prospect for the king's pleasure, and in the eighteenth century it was simply a walk through pastures and fields; in the first years of the nineteenth century it already hosted a few buildings; and by the second Empire it featured great hotels and luxurious estates. Today, boutiques, cafés, cinemas, airline offices, and the celebrated Lido are among the attractions of the most famous street in the world. The Champs-Élysées triumphantly reaches the Louvre, leaving on the right along the Seine the *rocaille* exuberance of the Pont Alexandre III and the scenic view of the Petit Palais and the Grand Palais. The latter are testimony to the era in which Paris, capital of science and technology, gathered together the nations of the world every ten years to celebrate the marriage of Progress and Reason.

84 top In these photos can be seen a number of views of the futuristic Quartier de la Défense, also known as "Wall Street-sur-Seine" in acknowledgement of the financial importance assumed over recent years by this area in the western suburbs of the city.

84-85 La Grande Arche de la Défense stands out in the western suburbs of the city in all its spectacular and clean-cut futuristic glory. The gigantic cube of white Carrara marble, over 100 metres tall, could comfortably contain the entire cathedral of Notre-Dame.

85 A symbol of challenge and modernity, La Grande Arche de la Défense, the work of the Danish architect Von Spreckelsen, was backed by President Mitterrand as the home of the International Foundation for Human Rights and as a monumental work commemorating the bicentenery of the French Revolution.

86-87 Stone lions, allegorical statues, grandiose lamp-posts, copies of those on the Trinity bridge in St. Petersburg, lend a magical, absolute beauty to the Pont Alexandre III that links the Esplanade des Invalides with the Champs Élyseés. The bridge was named after the Tzar of Russia Alexander III to mark the 1893 alliance between France and Russia and has a single span around 100 metres long. These photos exalt the wealth of the decorations and the stature of the lamp-posts illuminating the bridge as dusk falls.

Enlarged and partially reorganised at the behest of Mitterrand, the grandiose Louvre houses the largest collection of art in the world. To stroll among the statues of the Cour Marly in the Richelieu wing; to step back in time in front of the winged bulls of Korsabad, the *Venus de Milo*, and the *Winged Victory of Samothrace*; to plunge into the High Renaissance of Michelangelo, Raphael and Leonardo, then into the sixteenth century

Dutch still-lifes and the bucolic landscapes of Poussin and Watteau; and to admire the stunning, seemingly endless sequence of masterpieces in the Grande Galerie requires time, effort, and more than just one visit. Following the Mitterrand revolution, the entrance to the museum on the Rue de Rivoli has become a remarkable sight, with the inverted glass pyramid of architect Jeoh Ming Pei, drawing light from the larger, external pyramid serving as the principle entrance to the Louvre at the centre of the Cour Napoléon. Seen from below, the magical play of light and glass reflects the clouds and the silhouettes of tourists who seem to be suspended in mid-air, actors in a surreal world, while the Parisian sky penetrates the hazy transparency of the glass, and sheds its silvery light upon the inverted pyramid below.

88-89 The new Louvre created in the heart of the city, seen here in an aerial view, throws a new light on immortal masterpieces such as the Winged Victory of Samothrace, *top right, and the* Venus de Milo, *bottom left.*

90 The entrance
to the New Louvre
is located below
the glass pyramid
designed by
the Chinese-American
architect Jeoh Ming

Pei and built in the
centre of the Cour
Napoléon, but the
museum can also
be reached via Rue
de Rivoli via the
Carrousel du Louvre.

91-94 The
Mitterrand era
changed the face of
Paris. Among
the grands travaux
initiated by
the celebrated
President was
the transformation
of the Louvre

complex, beginning
with the inauguration
of the pyramid
in the middle of
the Cour Napoléon
and continuing with
the opening of the
Richelieu wing and
the reorganisation
of the Denon wing.

95 The spacious, well-lit halls of the Louvre contain masterpieces from all eras and from all over the world. The world's greatest museum can in fact boast works of art dating back as far as 5,000 years B.C. as well as contemporary pieces.

97 Here the work is surrounded by Jan Vermeer's The Lace-maker, Raphael's portrait of Baldassare Castiglione, Eugène Delacroix's Liberty leading the people *and Camille Corot's* Dame en bleu.

96 *Among the innumerable masterpieces to be found within the Louvre, the sweetly enigmatic smile of Leonardo da Vinci's* Mona Lisa *stands out.*

98 top On one side of the Place de la Concorde, towards the Tuileries and the Louvre, stands the Arc de Triomphe du Carrousel built at Napoleon's behest in 1806 and topped at that time by a copy of the celebrated horses from the Basilica of San Marco in Venice.

At the end of the Cour Napoléon, the Arc de Triomphe du Carrousel, with its eight columns of pink marble, frames the celebrated view of the Champs-Élyseés. Bucolic in the shade in the Tuileries gardens, yet regal in the vast arena of the Place de la Concorde, this is the setting for well known celebrations, funeral processions and military parades. The obelisk, from the temple of Luxor, was placed in the middle of this square in the autumn of 1836, at the site where, from 1793 to

1795, the inexorable guillotine brought thousands of people, including the minute, austere figure of Marie Antoinette, to meet their maker. Kings and queens also haunt the nearby church of Saint-Germain l'Auxerrois in the Place du Louvre which was once the parish church of the French sovereigns, patronised by Francis I, Henri IV, and Louis XIV, and dedicated to Saint-Germain, bishop of Auxerre.

100-101 The Centre
Pompidou rises in
the heart of the city,
and with its brightly
coloured tubes,
exposed steel tie-rods
and external
escalator enclosed in a
transparent Plexiglas

tube, its challenging
character has been
a source of
controversy ever since
it was built. It has
nevertheless become
the city's most
popular cultural
attraction.

100 top The futuristic
Centre Pompidou
faces onto the singular
Igor-Stravinsky plaza,
characterised by the
multi-coloured
animated fountain
designed by Niki de
Saint-Phalle and
Jean Tinguely.

100 bottom
Each day the broad
open space alongside
the Beauborg
provides a stage for
numerous street
artists who perform
for hurrying
Parisians and
fascinated tourists.

The nearby Musée des Arts Decoratifs
and the Musée des Arts de la Mode
take us on a trip through time, with
their packed rooms of antique furnishings: Louis XV furniture, tapestries, jewels, fabrics, ceramics, glass,
toys, rugs, objects from daily life,
lace, and sumptuous clothing belonging to famous figures of the past.
Nearby in the Jardin des Tuileries,
the Musée de l'Orangerie displays the
impalpable softness of Claude Monet's
Waterlilies, the solitary still-lifes of
Cézanne, Renoir's *Les Fillettes au
Piano*, a number of *Odalisques* by
Matisse and, between a Picasso and a
Modigliani, the unmistakable Parisian
scenes of Utrillo. The strangest, most
controversial, modern, and daring
museum of Paris comes into sight
suddenly at the corner of the Rue
Rambuteau. This is the Centre Pompidou, the famous Beaubourg, with
its improbable weaving of coloured
and transparent pipes and all those
steel rods. This building is the original
creation of architects Renzo Piano,
Gianfranco Franchini, and Richard
Rogers, and it has frequently been
likened to a coloured refinery, a
"modern idol of leaded Plexiglas, like
a space station in the heart of the
city." Visited annually by seven million people, the Beaubourg is an
ultra-modern, polyvalent cultural
centre which includes a huge library
of texts on figurative art and the
Musée National d'Art Moderne.

101 top "A unique original effort to unite and render accessible the various elements of modern culture in a single complex". This was the principal aim behind the most talked about and unusual of Paris's museums, inaugurated in 1977 and seen here in a stunning aerial photo.

102-103 The Centre National d'Art et de Culture Georges-Pompidou, better known as the Pompidou Centre or the Beauborg, contains the Museum of Modern Art in which you can admire works by the greatest artists of the century, almost all of them masterpieces that once hung in the Museum of Modern Art created in 1937 and the National Centre for Contemporary Art created in 1967. The collections are to be found on the fourth floor of the Pompidou Centre: it is here that you will find works such as The Muse by Pablo Picasso (large photo right), Lolotte by Amedeo Modigliani (top right), Georges Braque's Young Girl and guitar (top left) and Giorgio de Chirico's Premonitory portrait of Apollinaire (bottom). Alongside the works of these artists there are also those of the Fauve painters such as Pierre Bonnard and Henri Matisse, the Cubists including Picasso, Fernand Léger and Braque and the major movements from the First World War to the 1960s.

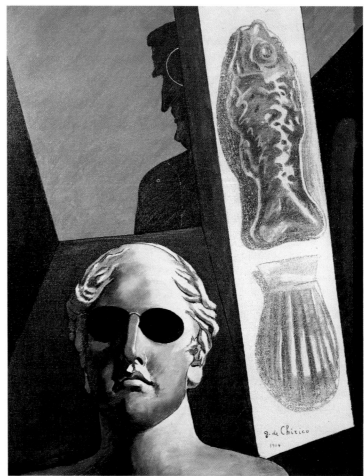

104 top Following a long period of neglect the Marais has been revived to experience a moment of explosive rejuvenation. It is now the most fashionable area of the capital, the quarter with the most museums, aristocratic buildings and trendy boutiques. Some of the streets have retained something of their original atmosphere, in others the old shops and commercial stores have given way to art galleries and the most sophisticated fashion houses of the moment. In this photo you can see a number of the sumptuous buildings facing onto Place des Vosges.

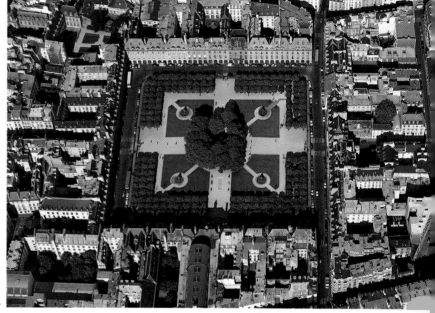

Behind it stretches the Marais, the ancient marsh that used to extend all the way from Place de la Concorde to the Bastille; today it is the most fashionable district of the city, with its narrow, elegant streets. For six hundred years, from the Dark Ages to the eighteenth century, this quarter of Paris was filled with the houses of the aristocracy, sumptuous apartments, churches, and convents. Place des Vosges is its most representative and enchanting corner. This royal playground was created for Henri IV initially as a garden for the *noblesse d'épée* (the ancient and noble art of swordsmanship). It is surrounded by red brick buildings with slate roofs that create an extraordinary symmetry, and is overlooked by an equestrian statue of Louis XIII and the spectres of famous personages that lived here: at number 6, Victor Hugo, whose house is today a museum of the relics and memories of the great writer; the Marquess of Sévignée, born at number 1, the Hôtel de Coulange. In adjacent streets stand other magnificent mansions: the Hôtel de Sens where the legendary Queen Margot, the wife of Henri IV, lived for a brief period; the Hôtel Salé, which since 1985 has been home to one of the most extensive collections of the works of Picasso; the Renaissance-style Hôtel de Sully, where temporary exhibitions are held; and the Hôtel Carnavelet, which contains the museum dearest to Parisian hearts. Here one loses oneself among salons, stairways and sumptuous furnishings, all records of history ranging from the Declaration of the Rights of Man to Voltaire's painting chair, from Proust's bedroom to Jean-Jacques Rousseau's inkpot, from the walking stick of Emile Zola to the original, antique keys to the Bastille.

106 top The Opéra Garnier, or rather the Opéra tout court as the Parisians say, is the Neo-baroque and eclectic palace that best expresses the architectural canons of the era of Napoleon III. The wealth of friezes, columns, domes, and bronze

and marble statues and the marriage of the classical and baroque styles create truly unique and overwhelming effect, so much so that the building has in the past been compared with an enormous, sophisticated cream cake.

106-107 Onto the perfect octagonal symmetry of the Place Vendôme face sumptuous homes and glittering shop windows. The square was designed by Jules Hardouin-Mansart and was destined to house a statue of Louis XIV.

107 top The daring and eccentric structure of the Opéra-Bastille houses one of the world's most famous ballet companies. This temple of music was inaugurated in 1989 and can accommodate 2,700 spectators.

107 bottom left This photo shows in detail the famous column that rises in Place Vendôme, erected at the behest of Napoleon Bonaparte as a tribute to a celebration of the Grande Armée.

107 bottom right The gilded Genius of Liberty stands atop the July Column, a monument over 50 metres tall in the centre of the Place de la Bastille and dedicated to the victims of the revolution of 1830.

One may go to the Place de la Bastille to admire the July Column erected in memory of the victims of the revolution of 1830, and the Opéra-Bastille, the great modern palace of concrete, marble and wood, the creation of Carlo Ott who has subverted the ancient concept of the theatre. "No longer horseshoe halls, no longer gilded candy bowls in which sound spins as if it were inside the body of a cello," writes Alessandro Baricco, "but mega-halls, enormous spaces, gigantic stages, thousands of seats, and multiple galleries." The right bank at the Place de la Concorde has become the epitome of luxury and supreme elegance. Gold and jewellery glitter in the shop windows of Place Vendôme, the architectural jewel created by Jules Harduin-Mansart for Louis XIV. At the end of Rue de la Paix is the ostentatious and Neo-baroque Opéra Garnier from the period of the Second Empire, and the Rue du Faubourg-Saint-Honoré which boasts the most exclusive shops. But you can already see the unmistakable profile of the Sacré-Coeur in the distance. At some point we all inevitably arrive here: this hill with its long flight of steps overlooking the roofs of the city, is where the Paris of myths still lives.

In a tree-lined square, garrisoned with artists ready to paint your portrait, with the brilliant whiteness of the church of the Sacré-Coeur, the blazing lights of the Pigalle, and the worn walls of the Bonne Franquette, it is still possible to imagine those roaring years in which Montmartre and brought forth its memorable contributions to art, and the outbursts of those restless, aimless youths of the most legendary bohemia.

108 top and 109 top Montmartre was the focus for a remarkable period in the history of the arts. An entire generation of artists contributed to the creation of its reputation: from Degas to Cézanne, from Delacroix to Monet and Van Gogh all of whom lived, suffered, painted and exalted here. However, few traces remain

of their presence. The early Bohème of Renoir and Lautrec was to be found at the top or the foot of the hill and 20 years later the likes of Picasso, Juan Gris, Van Dongen and Modigliani arrived to make their contribution to the legend of the quarter. Today the narrow streets swarm with people, mime artists, hawkers and buskers.

108 bottom There are numerous painters, especially in Place du Tertre, who attempt to revive the distant memories of a Montmartre that is no more.

108-109
The majestic white basilica of the Sacré-Coeur that dominates the hill of Montmartre was the fruit of a vow made by two businessmen, Alexandre Legentil and Rohault de Fleury at the beginning of the Franco-Prussian war of 1870: if France was to emerge victorious from the bloody conflict they would erect a church dedicated to the Sacred Heart of Christ. The work, under the direction of Guilbert — the city architect of the era — did not begin until 1875 and the church was not consecrated until 1919, following the victorious outcome of the First World War.

110 centre left
The Train Bleu
is the restaurant
at the Gare de Lyon,
the station from which
trains to the South
depart. For this
reason, in the great
stuccoed halls with
their gilded cornices,
19th-century frescoes
depict the most
famous tourist
destinations on the
Mediterranean
Riviera.

*110 bottom left
and right
The cafés of Paris
are not mere refuges
of conversation and
relaxation, some
of them, like the
Deux-Magots seen in
the photo bottom
right, have in fact
contributed to the
Parisian legend.*

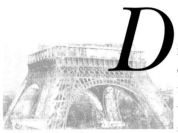

*110 top left The Café
de Flore is considered
to be the symbol
of a certain Paris;
the Flore was, in fact,
a permanent home
for Jean-Paul Sartre
and Simone de
Beauvoir during
the era of the
Existentialists.*

Divine Paris, an "immense shed of marvels, a theatre within the great theatre of the world": where to begin to share in the intimacy and spirit, emotions and charms, secrets and memories of this great capital of dreams? In the museums or during a walk along the Seine; in front of the latest, most controversial piece of architecture, or in a chic café on the Champs Élysées? Among the crowds on the boulevards or beneath the trees of the lonely Vert Galant? Walking, walking and more walking is the key to establishing an open dialogue with this city, which at every corner changes face and dimension, stirring one's memories and promising surprise. There is the Paris of history or the Paris of shopping, of art or of the joys of life, of wild nights or cosy bistros, the Paris of merchants or intellectuals, of the glittering shop windows or of the most improbable future, the Paris of long boulevards and the Paris of modernity. Within the great well of the city's golden history, dreams and fantasies, each of us finds our own beloved, unforgettable Paris, that mythical Paris we yearn to experience. Along the banks of the Seine, the serene and lofty river of poets and artists which divides the city into two worlds, the *bouquinistes* of the Rive Gauche, the oldest tenants of the Pont-Neuf, have been selling books and pamphlets since the seventeenth century. At night their goods are locked into cases of green-painted wood, an ancient custom which continues to this day, and one reproduced on countless postcards. In the gloomy half-light of Notre-Dame, pierced only by a few iridescent rays breaking through the stained glass windows, the ghosts of history may be perceived. Here Mary Stuart was married, Joan of Arc was proclaimed a

*111 Strolling along
the Champs Élysées
you will find cafés
offering an
opportunity to rest
in the leafy shade
of the trees lining
the boulevard.*

112 top left The display windows of Cartier, the celebrated Parisian jeweller, look out onto Rue de la Paix, the attractive street built for Napoleon in 1806, inaugurated in 1814 and named in commemoration of the peace treaty.

112 bottom left The Galeries Lafayette, close to the Opéra, is one of the most famous Parisian department stores. It started out quietly as a small boutique at the corner of La Fayette and Chausée-d'Antin and was expanded early in the 20th century.

112 right The interior of the Galeries Lafayette still features the balustrades attributed to Majorelle and an imposing glazed dome. Today the great store occupies a surface area of 120,000 square metres and is composed of three large inter-connected buildings.

saint, Abelard met the demure Eloise, and Napoleon crowned himself Emperor of France, wrapped in a pale brocade cloak embroidered with tiny golden bees. Little shops and restaurants, and Berthillon, the famous and historic ice-cream shop making the best ice-cream in Paris, all help to enliven the nearby Rue Saint-Louis-en l'Ile, an intimate street far removed from the Paris of broad spaces and conspicuous modernity. Saint-Germain-des-Prés is just a step away, on the left bank of the Seine, home to cafés in which pages of the legend of a certain Paris were once written, the Flore,

the Deux-Magots, and the brasserie Lipp. Here the ideas that stirred the hearts and souls of a generation were born. The powerful and rebellious atmosphere of the golden Sixties once thrived here, and Jean-Paul Sartre and Simone de Beauvoir were permanent fixtures at the Café de Flore, and with them their existentialist followers, unshaven in black turtleneck sweaters and wearing duffel coats rather than bourgeois overcoats. In the caves of this neighbourhood, the classic settings of this tumultuous world, Yves Montand and Juliette Gréco, dressed in black turtlenecks, were taking their first steps in what later became glorious careers. Today, the most stylish shopping streets branch off from the axis of the Boulevard Saint-Germain-des-Prés; luxury flirts with bohemia on Rue du Bac, Rue de Grenelle, and Rue de Sèvres, and fashion triumphs.

A world of fine antiques can be found a few blocks away along the Quai

113 The passages and the galeries are secret covered alleys that link two or more of the streets in a particular quarter. They were a very fashionable architectural feature early in the 20th century, partly because gas-lamps made them particularly attractive at night. These photos show the Passage Verdeau with its entrance at Number 6 Rue de la Grange-Batelière (top left) and the Galerie Vivienne, created in 1823.

Voltaire, the mythical *carré d'or* with all the unspoilt appeal of old Paris; the area bounded by the Rue de l'Université and Rue des Saints-Pères boasts nearly a hundred art shops. Montparnasse is in full sail at the end of Rue de Rennes, its bright, soaring mainmast represented by the vertiginous tower of glass and cement. This is an area bustling with life, that at night cloaks itself in the red lights of the more risqué shows, as well as the myriad lamps of the bistros (including the renowned Coupole and Dômme, the former favourites of the likes of Mirò, Picasso, Hemingway and Chagall). However that world of energetic *filles de joie*, young models with painted flowers on their calves and watches saucily attached to their garters, is far away. Remote is the world of *Kiki*

of *Montparnasse*, the quarter's symbol immortalised in the photographs of Man Ray. His nude portraits of her have found their way into museums all over the world. At the beginning of the century Montparnasse took the place of Montmartre, another legendary temple of a bygone Paris: the bohemian Paris of a hundred years ago coloured with love, avant-garde art and contradictions. In 1887 Degas, Cézanne, Monet, and many other artists lived upon the hill dominated by the Sacré-Coeur basilica. They were all friends and met at the Place du Tertre and danced together at country fairs in front of the Moulin de la Galette. In the same era, at the window of his room on Rue Lepie, Vincent van Gogh painted the roofs of Montmartre. Today Montmartre exists in flux between memory and consumerism, old quarters and new restaurants, false and authentic artists, the Moulin Rouge and Pigalle, and the heritage of those memories left upon the stubby hill — the *butte*, that has the Place de Tertre as its fulcrum — by a generation of legendary artists. You climb upwards, as if on a pilgrimage, to search for a world of memories, to gaze from above upon the grey roofs of Paris and the immobile sails of the Moulin Rouge, the mythical haunt of Montmartre's prime.

You then descend again and begin another tour, a hunt for another facet of Paris, to be found in the havens of taste, custom and tradition.

A trip to Paris is inconceivable without an excursion to its shops, boutiques, and most famous stores. In the sumptuous lounge of Faubourg Saint-Honoré or in the windows of the *triangle d'or*, reigns the world of haute couture and the most prestigious fashion houses. On the élite Place Vendôme, or scenographic Rue de la Paix, the window displays ooze luxury and extreme elegance.

Behind the Opéra, you will find the colourful bustle of the most famous department stores. These are located along the grandiose boulevards designed by Baron Haussmann under Napoleon III — a new, modern and imperial city built atop the flattened remains of the romantic and baroque medieval Paris.

The appeal of the old Marais, the city's Jewish quarter and today the most fashionable district in Paris, has been retained intact in its maze of narrow streets and rash of trend-setting boutiques grouped around the Place des Vosges, the most romantic and celebrated of the city's squares. Here one finds fascinating little museums devoted to the secret treasures of past lives (the Museum of romantic life, the Edith Piaf Museum, dedicated to the fragile and magnetic French *chanteuse*, and the Museum of merry-go-rounds and theatre design). There is also the alluring weekend market of Saint-Ouen, the largest flea market in the world, where you can roam for hours amongst the secrets of time past.

But Paris would not be Paris if, at sunset, the lights of a romantic restaurant, the colourful buzz of a brasserie, the sequins and spangles of the irresistible Folies-Bergère, or the artful rite of the eternal can-can did not take centre stage.

117 top It was the Pont-Neuf, the jewel of town-planning built at the behest of Henri IV, that housed the first book-sellers, the bouquinistes, who still today represent one of the best-loved postcard images of Paris. Along the banks of the Seine, close to the Pont-Neuf and the Cathedral of Notre-Dame they display second-hand books and old prints and postcards which they lock into typical green-painted wooden containers hung on the parapets along the river at night.

118 top The broad expanse of the Champ de Mars is all the more evocative at night when skilful lighting emphasises the great spaces and the solid structure of the École Militaire. On the left of the photo you can see the gilded dome of the Hôtel des Invalides.

118 bottom These aerial photos reflect the great harmony and monumentality of Paris and allow the historic quarters to be identified.

118-119 This spectacular nocturnal photo shows the Bastille, the centre of a new revolution in a quarter with a wealth of craft workshops, cafés and bistros that have grown up around the controversial Opéra-Bastille. At the centre of the square, where a 50-metre column now rises, once stood the famous fortress-prison of the Ancien Régime stormed on 14th of July, 1789, at the very start of the French Revolution.

*119 top
The unmistakable
sign of the Paris
Metro at Porte
Dauphine, known
as the Libellule,
is a splendid
example, the last
remaining,*

*of the creative genius
of Hector Guimard,
the father of French
Art Nouveau who
early this century
designed these
remarkable entrances
for the underground
railway system.*

*120-121 Paris,
the romantic city
par excellence, reveals
all its appeal
and mystery in this
photograph.*

VERSAILLES: GOLD-LEAF, MIRRORS AND ABSOLUTE POWER

122 top Reflected in the central pool, the main body of the Palace of Versailles is revealed in all its glory.

122 bottom The Temple of Love, created for Marie Antoinette, is enclosed in the dense vegetation of the park of Versailles.

122-123 The architecture of the entire Versailles complex was intended to be the highest expression of regal opulence. It was built for Louis XIV who fell in love with the design of the architect Le Vau to the extent that when the palace was almost completed he transferred his court there from Paris. The King himself personally oversaw the work of the landscape gardener Le Nôtre who was responsible for the design of the green areas such as the great lawn and the parterre to the north planted with flowers and box hedges.

Beyond the gilded gateway opens the door to an epoch marked by the glories of the French monarchy at its height. The forest of mirrors, the immense staircases, the silk-lined salons, damask curtains and gigantic crystal chandeliers have witnessed processions of courtiers, princes, high prelates and ambassadors, come to pay homage to the Sun King. Far away under the arch of the Salon de la Paix, the King sat solemnly on a throne three metres tall, set on a carpet of gold. The Marquess of Sévigné described the palace of Versailles as "a regal beauty unique in the world."

At every step the palace reminds you of the infinite power wielded by Louis XIV and his successors. In 1623 the joy of hunting, of the woods, and fresh, fragrant air, and the satisfaction of an overflowing game bag, led Louis XIII to build, in this place, a *pavillon de chasse*, later transformed into a larger edifice, the *petit château de cartes* of stone and brick, traces of which can still be seen in the facade of the Cour de Marbre, which has remained almost completely intact to this day. In 1661 Louis XIV, reluctant to demolish his father's favourite hunting lodge, decided to transform it into a much larger complex with the help of the architect Le Vau. The work begun then was to last until the end of his reign. At the beginning the King used the small castle as a secret refuge for his romantic dalliances with the beautiful Louise de la Vallière, and created a fairy-tale park around the hunting lodge, where he modelled nature after his dreams. And thus one summer night a stupefied court was invited to the unforgettable *Fête des plaisirs de l'île enchantée*, a great party in honour of the King's mistress which even Molière attended.

123 top Hundreds of statues are scattered throughout the immense park at Versailles. The gilded statues of Bassin di Latona (left) and the Apollon (right) are particularly stunning as they adorn the celebrated fountains and the pools in the great garden.

124 Louis XIV was obsessed with the Palace of Versailles and dedicated himself to the building throughout his reign. The apartments and the great halls such as the Salon de Diane (right) or the Opéra Royal (left) with the gallery decorated by Pajou reflect the continuous search for decorative splendour and opulence.

Extensions were then begun, and Versailles was transformed into a magnificent baroque palace, the King's finest achievement, his most eternal and admired invention. In 1666, after the death of his mother, Anna of Austria, Louis XIV began to consider Versailles more seriously as the principal residence for the sovereign and his court, a dream that was realised in 1682. This great complex, about twenty kilometres from Paris, became the most extraordinary *ville royale* in the world. Ten thousand courtiers (including five thousand noblemen) were fed in the court dining rooms every day. They surrounded the King, serving him with dignity and honour. From 1683 the King opened the doors of his apartments to his court, hosting dances, games, and spectacles for their amusement. If in 1661 the little village of Versailles was just a handful of houses in the country, by 1713 it was a town of forty-five thousand inhabitants; and the *ville nouvelle*, as it was known at

the time, was connected to Paris by an incessant coming and going of horses, carriages, and carts. The immense estate that enclosed the palace in a great green lung was surrounded by a wall around forty kilometres long, with twenty-four monumental gates (of which only five remain today). Only a small part of the primitive park remains but it is still magnificent.

It was Louis XIV's constant preoccupation throughout his reign. He found the ideal interpreter and accomplice for his most fantastic projects in Le Nôtre, the celebrated architect of the gardens. Le Nôtre conceived for the king not a garden, but rather a baroque city, full of surprises, in which the most fertile imaginations were free to express themselves in the creation of the world's most extravagant parties... To realise this idea of a green city, Le Nôtre modelled nature as though it were a theatre, resorting to every type of visual trick, great screens of trees and numerous little woods growing in every corner enclosing mythological statues, playful fountains, or unexpected labyrinths. He flooded the Grand Canal, upon which Venetian gondolas and a flotilla of miniature warships glided. The court remained at Versailles until 1789, when the Revolution forced Louis XVI to return to Paris. In the face the rebellion, on the dramatic night of 6th of October of that year he descended through a spectacular secret passage in the palace to rejoin his queen Marie Antoinette, who had already escaped by another route. Versailles

125 The photos on this page offer further glimpses of the interior of the palace and bear witness to the magnificence of the decorations completed for Louis XIV, his successor Louis XV, the only King to have spent his life and the years of his reign at Versailles, and Louis XVI. In the royal chapel, dedicated to St. Louis (centre) the harmony of the Neo-classical colonnade stands out.

The staircase that leads to the apartments of the Queen (bottom right), features beautiful inlaid marble whilst the Galerie des Batailles (top right), created in 1836 in the old apartments of the southern wing, is an important picture gallery containing works depicting the great battles that belong to the Musée de l'Histoire de France, established in the 19th century.

126 left Pure gold is the key motif in the splendours of the royal palace. In this photo you can see a detail of the decoration of the panelling designed by Richard Mique in 1783 for the Queen's cabinet doré.

126 top These photos depicting some of the interiors of the Palace of Versailles, provide clear evidence of the boundless luxury of the King's apartments and in particular the Salon de l'Oeil de Boeuf (left) and Marie Antoinette's chamber (right).

126-127 This photo allows us to wallow in the luxury of the royal apartments. It was in this sumptuous room that King Louis XIV, the Sun King, died in 1715. Elegant gilded friezes, brocades and precious tapestries are features of what was from 1701 the King's bedchamber. The ceremony of the lever du Roi *took place in this room each morning as the members of the royal family and the courtiers paid homage to the sovereign.*

127 While it took half a century to construct the Palace of Versailles for the Sun King, it took a further 20 years, different kings and much work to bring it to that pitch of magnificence enjoyed by all those who pass through the gilded entrance gates today. In this photograph can be seen the Queen's chamber decorated by two famous masters, Jacques and Jacques Ange Gabriel during the reign of Louis XV. The chamber is preceded by an antechamber known as the Grand Couvert *with a heavily decorated ceiling.*

was ransacked and soon fell into ruins, as did the park and all its marvels, until 1837 when the Chamber of Deputies declared Versailles a museum. Thanks to the American patron Rockefeller, a restoration of the complex was undertaken after the First World War, and was continued by the French government after 1952. Thus, today, the halls and salons can recount their magical history rendered all the more exceptional by some quite breathtaking figures: a surface area of 800 hectares, 330,000 plants, 375 windows facing onto the enormous garden whilst at the service of this "factory of marvels" are 70 gardeners, 200 guards, 12 firemen, and 400 members of the general staff. The palace receives nearly 5 million visitors per year.

Having passed through the perimeter wall, the immense construction unfolds in all its splendour. Rigorous order was imposed at Versailles: the princes and other dignitaries lived in the north and the south wings, facing the garden, while the courtiers had their apartments by the village.

The royal apartments were found on the first floor of the main building — the King to the north, and the Queen to the south. They were reached by two marble staircases, that of the ambassadors which no longer exists and that of the Queen. Behind the Cour des Ministres, bounded by balustrades and featuring an equestrian statue of Louis XIV and memories of Montgolfier and Pilâtre de Rozier's early ballooning experiments, lies the Royal Court, which only the carriages of the royal family and ministers reached. Then comes the Cour de Marbre, with its traces of the original castle of Louis XIII, and the King's bed chamber at the centre. The Opéra, a building constructed for the wedding of Louis XVI and Marie Antoinette of Austria in just one year (1770), is the architect Gabriel's masterpiece. The long western facade of the palace, which one reaches via the Cour Royale, extends a full 580 metres. Inside are rooms dedicated to Louis XIII and Louis XIV, with portraits of kings, queens, court favourites and famous personages. There is the grand apartment of the monarch, composed of six ceremonial rooms, and the Hall of Mirrors — Versailles

*129 top left The small
apartments had
a private character
and it was here that
Louis XIV kept and
admired the
masterpieces in his art
collection such as the
Mona Lisa. The photo
shows the Cabinet de
la Pendule that owes
its name to the
astronomical clock
that can be seen in the
background.*

*129 top right
The official life
of the court took place
in the great
apartments, here can
be seen the Salon du
Mercure. Beginning
with the Salon du
Hercule, each
apartment is
dedicated to a Greek
divinity.*

*128 This miniature
theatre was built for
Marie Antoinette
towards the end of the
18th century and is
to be found in the
gardens of the Grand
Trianon.*

at its most theatrical — the genial
creation of Mansart from 1678 to
1686, with paintings by Le Brun.
Today the seventeen panels mirrored
with mercury, illuminated by as many
windows, reflect the figures of visitors,
but at the time of the Sun King they
reflected a roomful of precious furniture of pure silver set against the walls
of the long gallery. Other apartments
with the bedchambers of the various

*128-129 Louis XVI
had the Grand
Trianon, a
sumptuous palace in
stone and pink
marble, built in
1687 as a refuge
from the strict court
protocol.
This photo shows
the Salon des Glaces,
the hall in which
the King received
his ministers
and the members
of the royal family.*

kings that lived in the palace and
salons filled with treasures, silk tapestries and famous paintings lead to the
offices of Louis XV, masterpieces of
French decorative art and cabinet-
making. The queen's apartments fol-
low, with the room of the queen's
guard, the coronation hall, the apartment of the Dauphine and Dauphin,
and then, after this long exaltation of
power and luxury, you finally emerge
into the silence of the immense park.

The fountains run only from May to
September on scheduled Sundays,
and attract up to 20,000 visitors a day
to marvel at the play of the myriad
water features, and to take part in the
great night parties that re-evoke, at
Neptune's Pool, the spectacular celebrations at the time of the Sun King. To
the right of the Grand Canal, inside the
park, is the Grand Trianon, the work of
Le Vau, erected on whole hectares of
former pastures and villages which
were destroyed to make room for the
bon plaisir du roi. The Grand Trianon
stunned contemporary observers: "a
nothing, just a small thing crouched
between flowers, jasmine, oranges,
intimate and splendid," gracefully
ethereal. This ceramic *rêverie*, entirely
covered in white and blue porcelain,
was also a secluded refuge where the
king and the queen could repose in
intimacy. Today the ceramic has been
replaced by white and pink marble,
re-establishing the Grand Trianon as a
masterpiece of refinement. The *hameau
de la reine* was constructed here on
the banks of an artificial lake for Marie
Antoinette — this was an operetta village, a life-size puppet theatre, inspired
by Jean-Jacques Rousseau's call for a
return to nature. Nestling in the greenery not far away is the Petit Trianon,
five sumptuously furnished rooms and
a beautiful English-style garden, with
magnificent exotic and rare trees. This
was a favourite of Marie Antoinette,
but also the last residence of Madame
de Pompadour, the King's famously
influential lover.

130-131 This is the most symbolic, grandiose and spectacular view of the Palace of Versailles, the Galerie des Glaces illuminated by 17 great windows throwing light onto an equal number of arched mirrors. Scenes depicting episodes from the life of Louis XIV, here seen as an ancient hero, were painted on the ceiling by Le Brun.

INDEX

136 The warm embrace of the setting sun and the car headlights frame the Arc de Triomphe.